KNOW YOUR BIBLE SERIES

10

TIMOTHY
TITUS
JAMES
HEBREWS
PETER
JUDE

ROY L. SMITH

ABINGDON PRESS
NASHVILLE

Timothy, Titus, James, Hebrews, Peter, Jude

No. 209218

Printed in U.S.A.

INTRODUCTION

Down through the centuries the Christian Church has held firmly to the belief that the Bible is God's supreme means of communicating with the mind of man. As a result of this belief it has set the Scriptures at the very center of its faith in God.

This belief in the supreme function of the Scriptures has, however, given rise to many misconceptions concerning the processes by which the Bible has come down to us in its present form. In our effort to exalt its spiritual significance and pay tribute to the great truths which are to be found on its sacred pages, we have missed many basic facts concerning its origins and growth, with the result that we have also missed much of its power to fit us for the adventure of living as people ought to live who are made in the image of God.

Again and again it has happened that devout people, as they have read their Bibles, have found sentences, phrases, and even whole paragraphs leaping out at them as if they might have been printed in boldface type, conveying to them special messages for special needs. Such experiences remain forever thereafter as some of the richest memories of life. It is the persistent faith that God does speak to sincere seekers through its pages that sends humanity back to the Bible year after year and century after century in search of moral and spiritual guidance. And it is the testimony of the Christian Church through nearly seventeen hundred years that *the Bible has never failed to open the way to God*. It speaks to every generation, and to people under every condition and circumstance of life.

It is because the Bible was born out of the experiences of living people that it is able to minister to people who are struggling with the problems of life. The proof of its inspiration is its power to inspire.

There are, however, certain very human facts about the Bible which are just as real as the fact that the Spirit of God speaks through its pages. The person who understands these facts—physical, social, historical, and intellectual—is in the best position to appreciate the spiritual powers which are embedded in the Scriptures.

The book we hold in our hands, for instance, consists of sheets of paper which have been made by men's hands. It is printed with ink and type which men have made. The very first pages on which the sacred words were written were also the handiwork of men—very ancient men, of course, but men nevertheless. The hand that wrote those words down in the first place was a human hand; the words were taken from human speech, with all its limitations and variations. No matter how vividly and distinctly God appeared and spoke to the writers of Scripture, the message was filtered through a human mind before it reached other minds, and in that filtering process it was colored deeply by human experiences.

As soon as we approach the Bible with this in mind we discover that there is apparent a process of growth by which man's understanding of spiritual principles advanced from the primitive to the mature. The worshiper of Yahweh in the wilderness of Sinai was sincere and earnest, but his knowledge was limited. His first efforts to serve God were awkward because he was spiritually and intellectually in his infancy. But as he grew in knowledge and accumulated spiritual experience, he advanced beyond the childlike concepts with which he set out on his quest after God. Under the tutelage of prophets to whom God revealed himself, the Hebrew race rose to a spiritual eminence never attained by any other race of antiquity, and by the time Jesus was born the Jew was the most spiritually matured man on earth.

Similarly, a process of growth is clearly evident in the Christian Scriptures. True, the time period involved is very much less than in the case of the Old Testament, but the course of spiritual development is perfectly plain. In the writings which we study in this inquiry we may feel at times that we are witnesses of confusion only. Statements in the Pastoral Epistles may seem at variance with teachings of Hebrews, and both may differ from the judgments of Paul. But if we are to understand the New Testament as a whole, we must trace the gropings of the mind of the early Church as it struggled to comprehend the magnitude of the message which had been entrusted to it.

Roy L. Smith

4

Three Letters
and Five Tracts

1 What does this title mean?

It means that there are to be found in the New Testament a group of three letters, addressed to individuals, which are commonly known as the "Pastoral Epistles," and that there are also five brief treatises, written by various authors, which were designed to be circulated widely among Christians in something of the same way as a modern tract is used. The epistles were written for the purpose of strengthening the organization of the Church, but the tracts were in considerable part designed as propaganda material for the Christian movement.

2 Which are the Pastoral Epistles?

The two letters to Timothy and the one to Titus.

3 Which are the five tracts?

James, First and Second Peter, Jude, and Hebrews.

4 What does "pastoral epistle" mean?

Those great letters of the New Testament which are known definitely to be of Pauline authorship are all, with the exception of the letter to Philemon, messages addressed to churches. The Pastoral Epistles are communications addressed to two individuals—Timothy and Titus—who were expected to assume responsibilities somewhat similar to those of a modern pastor. The name "Pastoral Epistles" was first suggested by a great Christian scholar of the thirteenth century, Thomas Aquinas; but the expression did not come into common use until 1726, when Paul Anton, another famous scholar, used it and made it familiar to Bible students everywhere. In 1849 the illustrious English scholar Alford lent the weight of his endorsement to the title, and it is now used almost exclusively among students of the Scriptures. The name is entirely appropriate because the three books consist very largely of instructions to young pastors as to how to carry on the work of Christian congregations.

5 Who was Timothy?

He was a young man born of a mixed marriage in the city of
Lystra, in the province of Galatia. His father was a Greek (Acts
16:1), and his mother was a Jewess by the name of Eunice (II
Timothy 1:5). Many scholars believe the father must have died
sometime previous to our meeting with Timothy, for no
mention is made of him, and we do not even know his name. So
far as the New Testament records indicate, the family consisted
of Timothy, his mother Eunice, and his grandmother Lois.

6 Was he one of Paul's converts?

It is known that Paul made at least two visits to the city of
Lystra (Acts 14:6-23; 16:1-5) and that he made converts on both
occasions. In his letter to the Corinthian church (I Corinthians
4:15-17) Paul claimed Timothy as his "beloved and faithful
child," and such he probably was, in a spiritual sense, though
the record (Acts 16:1) is somewhat indefinite. It is generally
believed, however, that the family was converted on the
occasion of Paul's first visit to Lystra and thereafter represented
the more devout element of the congregation.

7 Was Timothy a Gentile?

As the son of a Greek father, he took his nationality, and must
have been numbered in the community as a Greek, and, of
course, as a Gentile, in spite of the fact that his mother was a
Jewess. But he seems to have been trained by his mother Eunice
in the Hebrew religious faith (II Timothy 3:15) without
becoming an actual Jewish proselyte.

8 How can we be so sure?

All Jewish male children were circumcised at the age of eight
days, this rite constituting their credential of membership in the
Jewish nation and their right to participate in the benefits of the
Jewish salvation. Any Gentile desiring to embrace the Jewish
religion was required to undergo this rite somewhat as a
modern man might be required to be baptized before he could
join a Christian church. We know that up to the time of his
meeting with Paul and his acceptance of the Christian faith,
Timothy had not been circumcised, for Paul states very

6

definitely that he performed the rite for him (Acts 16:3).

9 What does this signify?

It means that, though his mother was a Jewess and that he made his home with her, he was not recognized as a Jew in Lystra. No matter how well he may have been versed in Jewish beliefs, he remained, technically, a Greek, as his father had been. He was probably what was known as a Hellenized Jew.

10 What was a Hellenized Jew?

When Alexander the Great conquered the world (336–323 B.C.), he undertook to make it one vast Greek kingdom. All men were to speak the Greek language, be learned in Greek arts and culture, and think in terms of Greek ideas. He was so successful that, though his dynasty ran out and his political hopes failed, the life of the world was stamped indelibly with Greek thought and manners. Greek theaters and athletic shows were set up everywhere. In Paul's day Rome dictated the political life of the world and, incidentally, its economic life, but Greece ruled the world's mind and dictated its manners in large part.

Among all the ancients there were no people who mingled more freely with the world than did the Jews. Partly because of their commercial instincts, partly because they were members of a subject race, and partly because of the missionary impulse provided by their religion, the Jews went everywhere. There was no great city in the East which did not number among its population at least a small colony of Jews. In some cities there were thousands. In Alexandria, Egypt, they composed almost a third of the city's vast population. Literally millions of Jews were born outside of Palestine and grew up to speak the language of the land in which they were born. By a perfectly natural process they took on the culture and customs of the people among whom they lived. Being far removed from the Temple in Jerusalem, and able to attend only occasional feasts, it was inevitable that their loyalty would come under great strain and that they would relax some of the severities of their ritualistic observances. It is impossible to describe all the aspects of this liberalizing tendency, but by scholars it has been called "the Hellenizing process" and is understood to mean a blending of Greek philosophy and Jewish religion under the guise of liberalism.

11 Was a Hellenized Jew a renegade Jew?

Not at all. It is quite probable that he was in most respects the moral equivalent of an observant Jew of Jerusalem. But in observance of the ancient ritual he was at a very great disadvantage because he lived among Gentiles and could not maintain his ceremonial purity. The Jerusalem Pharisees, representing as they did the strictest sect, held all Jews outside the radius of the Temple observances under great suspicion, and any evidence of a liberal attitude was anathema to them. As some evidence of the loyalty of the Hellenized Jews toward the ancient faith and of the strength of their party in Jerusalem, however, there was a synagogue at which the Jewish services were conducted in Greek (Acts 6:9) for the convenience of Greek-speaking Jews who may not have been able to speak more than a few words of Hebrew. From the very first the Christian gospel had a very definite appeal for such.

12 How did the Christian faith appeal to the Hellenists?

While Jesus was yet alive he had at least one friendly hearing among them (John 12:20-21). Then on the day of Pentecost a considerable part of the audience which heard Peter was made up of Greek-speaking Jews, many of whom seem to have been permanent residents in Jerusalem. From almost the very first, Hellenistic Jews made up a considerable proportion of the Christian community, and they furnished the first Christian martyr—Stephen. To them Paul was able to speak on very intimate terms.

13 Why was Paul favored by the Hellenistic Jews?

In the first place, he spoke their language, having learned it as a boy in his home city of Tarsus, which was a Greek community (Acts 21:39; 22:3). He never was a Jerusalem Jew, but forever remained something of an alien in the city of David, even when he was a resident of the city and a persecutor of the Christians. When he became a Christian, however, he found he had much in common with the Greek-speaking Jews, and this made him the effective evangelist among them which he proved to be. This Greek background may have enabled him to reach Lois, Eunice, and the young man Timothy and bring them into the Christian movement.

14 How did Timothy happen to enter the Christian ministry?

In the case of Paul, the story of his conversion was recorded in considerable detail. Likewise his entrance into the ministry is described with due regard for historical facts. But in the case of Timothy we have no such record. All we know is that his mother and grandmother were women of marked piety (II Timothy 1:5). The book of Acts contents itself with the simple statement that Paul took Timothy with him (Acts 16:1-3) as a co-worker and companion, the young man having been found to enjoy an excellent reputation among the people of the Lystra church. Finding that the young man had never been circumcised, and knowing that this was certain to shut him out of Jewish homes and society as well as arouse much controversy and unnecessary strife, Paul performed the rite as a concession to Jewish consciences. From that time on we get frequent glimpses of Timothy as he worked in co-operation with Paul in various missions, sometimes being entrusted with responsibilities of very great importance. As one of Paul's converts (I Corinthians 4:14-17) and as a devoted Christian of some local reputation, he must have seemed like an ideal choice.

15 What were his responsibilities?

In the first place, the occasion of his being called to accompany Paul was marked by solemn ceremonies. The Apostle was not accustomed to making such decisions lightly or casually. The local leaders of the church arranged for a ceremony (Acts 13:3) in which they "laid their hands on" the young man and commissioned him for the work. In acknowledgment of their confidence, Timothy made a brief address in which he declared his faith (I Timothy 6:12-13) and may have been given the title of "evangelist" (II Timothy 4:5).

The first missionary journey into Europe found Timothy accompanying Paul and assisting him at Philippi, Thessalonica, and Beroea. When Paul left for Athens, Timothy remained behind for a while to observe the course of events. After a short time he followed on to Athens and rejoined Paul. In the meantime the Apostle became anxious about the state of affairs in Thessalonica and sent Timothy back to that city to get a report (I Thessalonians 3:1-6). The news he brought back was good, as we learned in our study of Thessalonians, and we next find him at Corinth (II Corinthians 1:19) and at Ephesus (I Timothy 1:3) as Paul's colaborer in the work of evangelism. At a somewhat later time he was sent as Paul's personal representative to compose the differences which were disrupting the Corinthian church (I Corinthians 4:17), a task in which he was not entirely successful. He was associated with Paul in some minor fashion in the composition of II Corinthians and was with him a second time in Corinth (Romans 16:21), as well as in his brief ministry at Troas (Acts 20:4 ff.). During Paul's imprisonment at Rome, Timothy served him as a personal companion in the furtherance of the gospel "as a son with a father" (Philippians 2:19-24).

16 Did he give his life to the ministry?

Like many another early Christian he appeared on the stage of affairs on numerous occasions, accepted difficult assignments, did the work to the best of his ability, and then disappeared without leaving any word concerning his personal fate. Such fragmentary information as we have, however, indicates that he must have given most of his time to the work of evangelism from the time of the dedication service in Troas, and that he was a man of forthright character—dependable, trusted, and of considerable ability. There is some reason to believe that his later years were spent in Ephesus and the surrounding territory serving as the supervisor of the Christian churches in something of the capacity of a "bishop." The author of Hebrews speaks of him as having been set at liberty (Hebrews 13:23)—from which it is assumed that he suffered an imprisonment—but concerning any such experience we have no information beyond surmises.

17 Was he an important member of the early Church?

The two letters we have in the New Testament which were addressed to him, whoever may have been their author, give the impression that he was responsible for administering the affairs of a considerable body of the Church at a time when it was becoming a bit complicated with officers, organizations, formal rules, and elaborate problems of procedure. It is altogether probable that the fact of his close association with Paul had the effect of increasing the respect in which he was held and of enlarging the scope of his activities and responsibilities for the administration of the work of the Church.

18 For what purpose were these letters written?

The author seems to have felt it necessary to give Timothy some very strict advice concerning Church administration. The sects were beginning to give trouble, and there seems to have been some special necessity for using great care in selecting local leaders who would not bring the cause of the Church into disrepute. From the epistles that bear his name it is very apparent that the young Church in which Timothy ministered was beset by many difficulties, the solution of which called for fine discernment and rare discrimination.

19 What were those disputes?

In some cases the controversies raged about the question of providing care for the Christian widows; in other cases it seems to have been some question of doctrine that was causing division among the people; in still other cases it was necessary to combat heresies of one form or another. It is quite possible that there had been open scandals in which officers of the Church had brought disgrace upon the Christians by their immoral conduct. Then there was always the necessity of combatting the influence of gross evils which saturated the life of the world about the Church.

20 Who wrote these letters to Timothy?

This question raises one of the most debated issues in the whole field of New Testament study, and at least three opinions must be studied: (1) There are those who believe that Paul wrote the letters to Timothy. (2) Then there are those who believe that some other person, whose identity is unknown, was the author. (3) A third opinion, which resembles both of the preceding opinions, is held by others. According to their belief, an unknown author took fragments of Paul's sayings and writings, wove them together into one connected whole, added some few comments of his own, and put them out under Paul's name.

21 What about Paul's authorship?

The statement is made very frankly and definitely in the

opening verse of each of the two letters (I and II Timothy) that Paul is the author. This fact cannot be dismissed lightly, and nothing less than the most convincing reasons can be accepted if the Pauline authorship is to be denied.

22 What kind of evidence could be acceptable?

If it could be shown, for instance, that Paul's name had been inserted sometime after the letters were written that would be, of course, very convincing argument. The student will remember that in Study Number Nine of this series it was learned that the name Ephesus did not appear in the earliest manuscripts we have of the book of Ephesians. But no such evidence exists in the case of the letter to Timothy.

If it could be shown that the early Church Fathers were in doubt about the question of authorship, that too would be very convincing evidence, but there is very little proof of this sort. Irenaeus, Tertullian, and Clement of Alexandria all say they are from the hands of Paul, and they were not so many scores of years away from the original writing.

If it could be shown that some of the statements in the letters could hardly have been made by Paul, that references in the letters cannot be fitted into any sketch of Paul's life thus far available to us, or that the text presents serious language difficulties if Pauline authorship is accepted, then that would be evidence which would have to be given very serious consideration.

If we are not to go on believing that Paul is their author, some very good reason indeed must be offered which will explain why an unknown author would take the liberty of using Paul's name, crediting him with their authorship when they are not, actually, his composition.

23 What about the first kind of evidence?

There is none such. The name of Paul, as the author of the two letters to Timothy, has been associated with these little books as far back as we have any record of them. So far as we know, no scholar of any standing will question that statement. They have *always* been called "Paul's letters."

24 What about the second kind of evidence?

It is entirely possible that there may have been some slight additions to the texts as they have come down through the years, but no Church Father has left any record of any doubt as to the Pauline authorship of the books in the original. It is true that some of the Church fathers raised some questions as to their spiritual values, but they did not question them on the grounds of their authorship.

25 What about an unknown author using Paul's name?

Historians and students of Greek literature are well acquainted with the fact that it was a common practice for writers in that day to compose letters, tracts, pamphlets, and even books on various public issues and interesting themes and ascribe them to famous personages. Two things explain this custom: (1) there was not the pride of authorship among ancient writers that exists among modern writers; and (2) there was no financial profit to the ancient writer, and he therefore had no property interest to protect by attaching his name to his writings. To compose a letter, book, or tract and use a famous name as its author was regarded as perfectly legitimate so long as in the belief of the real author he was true to the mind of the famous person and was faithfully interpreting his thoughts and viewpoint.

It would be somewhat like the case of a modern man who might attempt to write a discussion of modern politics, ascribing it to George Washington in the sincere belief that he was saying the things Mr. Washington would say under modern circumstances.

This was done, apparently, in the case of Plato. Few scholars of the Greek classics would attempt to maintain that the great philosopher wrote all thirty-five of the dialogues which bear his name in the famous collection ascribed to him. If such a situation could have come about in the case of Plato's writings, it is argued, what could have prevented something like it in the case of some of Paul's writings?

26 Would it not have been dishonest?

We would consider it so if it were done for the sake of personal gain, honor, or prestige. But it was not done for any such purpose. Besides, our concepts of honesty have improved in the case of literary productions, just as progress has been made in other moral matters. We learned, for instance, that the

13

book of Philemon does not even suggest by so much as one word any thought that slavery is wrong, probably because the institution was never questioned in Paul's day. Everyone accepted it, including the slaves. But since that day we have come to a more discriminating judgment, and we have a conscience in the matter whereas the ancients had none. So also in the case of questions of authorship we have a more sensitive conscience.

27 Would any Christian have dared do such a thing to scripture?

We must remind ourselves at this point that no Christian of that day had any thought that these letters (or any other letters included in our New Testament) were scripture. They were purely private property and could be dealt with as such. It is a common practice, for instance, for the editors of modern hymnbooks to change a word or even a line here and there without any thought of dishonesty, especially if they think they can improve the expression or even the thought of the hymn. No one thinks of a hymn as having been "inspired," so that it cannot be changed without doing violence to its "inspiration." Neither did the early Christians think that they were tampering with scripture when they were handling the letters of Paul.

Even more, a devout Christian who possessed some notes and fragments of letters Paul had written would not feel he was doing anything dishonorable if he put these together in a more or less connected fashion, adding sentences of his own here and there to make them hold together, and then calling the whole a "letter" of Paul's. This would be especially true if he were confident that in so doing he was true to the mind and thought of Paul. He would be doing it for the good of the cause and for no personal profit or fame. In all this discussion we must remember that it was not until more than a hundred years after the letters to Timothy and Titus came into existence that they were called scripture. Until that time they could be handled with considerable liberty without doing them any injustice.

28 What about the fourth kind of evidence?

It is here that we find evidence that deserves the most careful consideration. Those who believe Paul could not have written the Pastoral Epistles base their opinions on five major premises:

14

(1) the epistles make use of a definite vocabulary; (2) they have their own peculiar theology; (3) the personal attitude of the author does not seem to be Pauline; (4) conditions inside the Church do not correspond to those of Paul's time; (5) there is contradictory historical evidence within the epistles.

29 What about the vocabulary of the Pastoral Letters?

In style and vocabulary all three epistles are very similar, indicating a common authorship, but in these same respects they vary greatly from authentic Pauline writings: (1) A number of strong words which appear frequently in the Pastoral Epistles do not appear anywhere in any writings known positively to be Pauline. For instance, the phrase "God our Savior" appears five times in the epistles (I Timothy 1:1; 2:3; Titus 1:3; 2:10; 3:4) and nowhere in any Pauline letter. (2) Instead of the compact and vigorous style which characterizes Paul's normal writing, these books contain series of verbose sentences loosely constructed and strung together with little concern for sequence or logic. In the opinion of careful students of literature this is very convincing evidence.

30 What about the theology of the epistles?

Whoever composed the Pastoral Epistles very evidently believed he was faithful to the Pauline system of thought, but in spite of that belief he distorts it in these little books. Paul, for instance, thought of faith and action as a unity. The believer surrendered his life to Christ and a new moral activity was a natural result. This meant that faith and morality were in essence the same thing. In the letters to Timothy and Titus, however, we come upon a different concept. Here the author believes that both faith and morality are necessary components of the Christian life but that they are separate from one another. The Christian is one who has surrendered to Christ, but he is also one who must make a constant effort to live a good life. Whereas Paul thinks that faith produces morality, the author of Timothy and Titus believes that moral conduct is an achievement entirely separate and of itself toward which a Christian must strive if he discharges his responsibility as one who believes in Christ. He seems to believe that a man's faith may be sure and his conduct doubtful, or that his conduct may be above criticism and his faith uncertain. The proper combination of the

15

two in a worthy Christian life he calls "godliness," and he writes the epistles in the hope that he may be able thereby to encourage "godliness."

31 What about the personal attitude of the author of the epistles?

Those who question the Pauline authorship of the Pastoral Epistles call our attention to the fact that the personal attitude of the author does not seem to fit into our understanding of Paul. The two men to whom the epistles are addressed—Timothy and Titus—were among Paul's most intimate friends and acquaintances. The letters are concerned with an extremely personal theme—their administration of the affairs of the churches. It would seem natural to assume that Paul would have written an intimate, genial, friendly and highly personal letter, at least as much so as in the case of the letter to Philemon. Instead, the writer is almost formal. In the opening words of First Timothy he begins by declaring himself an "apostle" (as if the recipient of the letter did not know, or did not admit, his status as such). At times he is almost patronizing in his tone, and some of the advice sounds as though he might doubt the dependability of the men to whom he was writing. Certainly this does not sound like Paul. There is being laid upon these two men the heaviest obligation imaginable, so far as the Christian movement is concerned, and under such circumstances it would seem almost impossible for Paul to have written at such length without expressing his glowing personal affection in some way.

32 Are the basic ideas of the epistles Pauline?

It is at this point that we meet one of the most difficult problems for the one who believes they were written by Paul. In Question 30 one phase of the matter was suggested, but there are also other aspects. In all other letters ascribed to Paul, the Apostle lays great emphasis upon the Christian doctrine of an inward fellowship with Christ which, he declares, is the right and privilege of every Christian. Indeed, he seems to assume that such a relationship is the distinguishing characteristic of a Christian. This is the basic theme of all his best writing, but in the letters to Timothy the emphasis is not upon the inward spirit but upon outward performances and conduct. Faith is not an attitude of the will but an intellectual assent to certain doctrines. In the authentic letters of Paul, the Christian is expected to *be* something, whereas in the letters to Timothy and Titus the Christian is expected to *believe* something, and then strive after moral character. In many cases the writer of the epistles uses Paul's words and phrases but imputes to them meanings which Paul never gave them in any other writing.

33   What about the conditions inside the Church?

In the years when the great Apostle was driving himself up and down across the empire, preaching the gospel, there was no official, or ordained, ministry in the Christian Church. Every believer felt he had the right, if he were moved by the Spirit, to preach wherever he could secure an audience. The original eleven disciples enjoyed a favored status not shared by any other—Paul had to fight for his status—and their words were accepted as having unique authority. But outside that limited circle all Christians stood on equal footing, enjoyed the same status, shared the same rights, and were at liberty to assert the same authority. All could claim the endorsement of the Spirit. Gifted men capable of effective public speech and moved by great convictions traveled far and wide preaching the faith as they believed it and making converts. The little congregations of Christians called themselves "brethren" and were called by their neighbors the people of "the Way" (Acts 9:2; 19:9, 23; 22:4) in token of the fact that they lived differently. No one recognized any differences of rank or distinctions of place among them. The Church was a brotherhood.

In the letters to Timothy and Titus, however, we came upon an entirely different situation. The Church has developed by this time and has an ecclesiastical system. It is primitive and simple, of course, but it has all the elements of a system nevertheless. There are preachers and evangelists, of course, but there are also "bishops," "elders," "deacons," and other officials whose duties seem to be more or less well defined. Whereas in Paul's day the gospel was preached by traveling evangelists and missionaries, now we seem to find settled pastors and organized churches. Evidently a great change has taken place inside the Church.

34 What about the historical records in the Pastoral Epistles?

These include the references to the officers of the Church, mentioned in the foregoing paragraph, of which there were five groups—bishops, elders, deacons, deaconesses, and widows. While it is true that Paul provided for local leaders on some occasions (Acts 14:23), and that there are definite traces of officialdom in the churches at Thessalonica and Corinth (I Thessalonians 5:12; I Corinthians 5:1-5), the situation reflected in the Pastoral Epistles seems much more advanced, as though considerable time had elapsed during which the system had grown.

35 Who and what were the bishops?

It is difficult for the modern churchman to think of "bishops" as anything but church officers of very superior rank, but as they are referred to in the Pastoral Epistles (I Timothy 3:2-7; Titus 1:7-9) one gets the impression that they had not yet come to such exalted position. Timothy and Titus are instructed to choose them, supervise their work, discipline them if necessary, and hold them to a strict account. The word "bishop"—*episkopos*—in Greek meant one who was called to preside over meetings and exercise some degree of oversight over the churches. It probably had no more official significance at the time the Christians took over the word than the modern word "chairperson." We must remember that the Christians did not invent these words as titles for their officers, but that they took over words in common use and applied them to their workers.

36 Who were the elders?

Among the Jews the word "elder" meant one who had earned the right to counsel the people. It may have come about by the increase of his years, by his reputation for wisdom or piety, or because he occupied some office. The seven "rulers of the synagogue," for instance, were called elders because of their office. The oldest member of the family had a certain right to represent his house in meetings where opinion was to be expressed or a vote was being taken. The "elders" of the Christian Church seem to have been men somewhat after that order.

37 Who and what were the deacons?

The word was in common use among the Greeks as meaning

a servant with varied duties but without official dignity. In at least one reference we find a hint that a deacon in the Church might rise to a higher dignity on the basis of merit (I Timothy 3:13), but the process by which he might rise is not described.

38 What were the duties of the different officers?

Bishops (I Timothy 3:2-7; Titus 1:7-9), elders (I Timothy 5:17-19; Titus 1:5-6), and deacons (I Timothy 3:8-10, 12) are mentioned in the epistles, but there is no outline of their duties, nor are there any distinctions in their rank which give us an adequate basis for evaluating the organization of the early Church. We do not know how the officers were chosen (unless they were appointed by Paul, Timothy, Titus, or other leaders), but we do know that Timothy was warned that he must use discretion in supervising them. How many such officers there were in any local church is not even hinted. About the most we can say is that the ecclesiastical system was well on its way (Acts 14:23; 15:2, 22-23; 20:17,28; Philippians 1:1).

39 What about the deaconesses?

There may have been instances in which gifted women rose to positions of leadership by the sheer power of their own personality (Romans 16:1), but in other cases the wife of a deacon was expected to qualify for service (I Timothy 3:11) by exhibiting unimpeachable morals and unquestioned integrity.

40 What about the widows?

One of the distinguishing characteristics of the early Church was its concern for the poor. The first charity of the Church was exercised in behalf of widows (Acts 6:1-2) who were included in the membership. There seems to be some reason to believe that the early churches had a list of all dependent widows who had a right to expect assistance from the Church and who were past sixty years of age. On occasions individuals were selected from among them for some special duty. Paul advised younger widows to marry (I Corinthians 7:8-9), perhaps as a means of relieving the local congregation of responsibility for their care. One of the first controversies within the infant Church was a dispute between Jerusalem Jews and the Hellenistic Jews concerning the provisions made for the care of widows, it being the complaint of the Hellenists that their widows were being neglected (Acts 6:1). The problem of caring for them seems to have been a matter that called for careful supervision and the exercise of some discipline. The very fact that Timothy was required to look into the situation indicates that it constituted an important function of church activity.

41 Do the facts of the Pastoral Epistles fit into Paul's life?

It is just here that we come face to face with the extremely difficult problem. The Pastoral Epistles mention several historical circumstances which, if accepted as facts, make it necessary for us to revise a considerable section of the record of Paul's life.

42 How can this be?

The Pastoral Epistles mention visits to Ephesus (I Timothy 1:3), Miletus (II Timothy 4:20), Troas (II Timothy 4:13), Crete (Titus 1:5), and two other possible preaching missions (II Timothy 4:10) of which we have no knowledge from other sources. This does not mean, of course, that no such visits could have been made, for we know full well that the book of Acts is not a complete record of Paul's activities; but it is extremely difficult to fit these movements of the Apostle into the life of Paul as we know of it from the book of Acts and the writings of Paul.

The student will remember that our study of Philippians left Paul in prison in Rome, where he was awaiting trial. We know, too, that he seemed to anticipate a release (Philemon 22; Philippians 2:19-24). In the book of Acts it is reported that he told the leaders of the church at Ephesus that they would never see his face again (Acts 20:25), and yet one gets the impression from the Pastoral Epistles that he did see them again. In the book of Acts it is reported that when Paul left Ephesus for Macedonia he sent Timothy on before him (Acts 19:22), but in First Timothy we are told that Paul left Timothy to supervise the work in Ephesus while he proceeded to Macedonia.

43 What is the explanation?

The charge upon which Paul was being held in Rome,

following his arrest in Jerusalem, was a pretty vague one. Had Paul not appealed his case to Caesar he might have been released (Acts 26:32). It is difficult to believe that he was put to death for no more serious crime than that of being involved in a Temple riot in Jerusalem. Many scholars are of the opinion that he was released from his Roman imprisonment after a few years and that when he found himself free again he visited Ephesus and other communities mentioned in the Pastoral Epistles. There is nothing in the authentic letters of Paul which would make such a turn of affairs impossible, and there are certain very old (but unproved) traditions which support the suggestion.

44 Does a trip to Ephesus seem probable?

We know that when he wrote his letter to the Romans he was en route to Jerusalem with the collection and that he had plans for proceeding from Jerusalem to Rome and on to Spain. If the theory that he was released from his Roman imprisonment is correct, we would have to assume that he changed his plans while in Rome and that he visited the eastern churches once more before setting out on his voyage to Spain. This would make room for a missionary journey to Crete and Dalmatia (II Timothy 4:10) of which we have no other record, and also provide an explanation for the cloak and books that were left at Troas.

45 Did not Paul die in a Roman prison?

This is the commonly accepted belief among the scholars, but it would not have been necessary that he die during his first imprisonment in Rome. He might have been arrested a second time and have died during a second incarceration. Some support is given this theory by certain statements in the Pastoral Epistles themselves.

46 How do the Pastoral Epistles support the idea?

We know that in the period of his first imprisonment he continued hopeful of a speedy release (Philemon 22; Philippians 2:19-24). But in the letter to Timothy he is represented as being almost completely hopeless (II Timothy 4:6-7).

47 What may we conclude about the question of authorship?

There seem to be at least four conclusions of which we can be reasonably sure: (1) The question cannot be settled positively on the basis of the evidence available. (2) Whether Paul wrote the epistles or not, we must conclude that the record we have of his life and work is not complete and that there were missionary journeys made of which we have no formal record. (3) Whoever wrote the epistles made use of Pauline words, phrases, and at least some ideas. (4) Regardless of the identity of the author we get an extremely interesting picture of the Christian Church and the problems it faced during the years that followed Paul's ministry.

In view of all the facts in the case, many scholars of standing believe that the Pastoral Epistles were written by some admirer of Paul's who made use of much Pauline material in writing the books, which he hoped might serve a very definite purpose in the Christian movement. In so doing he used the name of Paul in the belief that he was true to Paul's thought, and he addressed the letters to Timothy and Titus because they were recognized leaders in the Church.

48 For what purpose were the Pastoral Epistles written?

The message is perfectly plain, whoever the author may be, as soon as we consider six facts concerning the situation inside the Christian Church: (1) Timothy and Titus, following Paul, are the responsible leaders of the Christian churches. (2) The entire Christian movement is bedeviled by sects and cults growing up within it. (3) There is great need that the first organization shall be right for that will determine the whole course of Church history. (4) At least a few principles of organization are of fundamental importance. (5) The young administrators are to be instructed in their duties and warned against dangers that are sure to arise. (6) There are certain personal matters which must be discussed. To serve these six needs the three letters were written.

49 By whose authority were Timothy and Titus put in charge?

By the authority of Paul. At the time of his death he was the outstanding personality in the Christian movement, and his influence seems to have been powerful enough to enable him to confer authority on Timothy and Titus. His was not a leadership that had been conferred upon him by any popular vote, but the authority that naturally gravitates to a powerful personality. There was no world-wide organization or council of any kind empowered to choose leaders, and any authority the two young men may have had must have come from a more or less private arrangement between them and the great Apostle.

50 What about the authority of the eleven disciples?

The authority of the original disciples carried weight in the infant Church, of course, and the charge that Paul was not a member of that band was used against him with great effect on several occasions, as we learned in our studies of Corinthians and Galatians. But there had come a time when the work among the Gentiles had been parceled out to Paul and the work among the Jews reserved to the eleven (Acts 15; Galatians 2:9ff). Under this arrangement Paul's power grew as the Greek wing of the Church increased. By the time of his death his authority was well-nigh supreme among the Gentile churches. With the destruction of Jerusalem by the Romans in A.D. 70 the Jewish wing of the Church began a steady decline and figures less and less in Christian history.

51 What about the sects in the young Church?

The very nature of the Christian faith exposed it to serious hazards. It was a "religion of the Spirit," and held to the belief that the Holy Spirit of God spoke directly to the heart of each believer. This opened the way for individuals with strange ideas to claim divine sanction for their vagaries. On one occasion Paul made the question of individual guidance a test of discipleship (Romans 8:9), but it is easy to see how such a doctrine put the Church at the mercy of irresponsible individuals who claimed to be believers. We have seen how the Galatian church was threatened by heretics (see study of Galatians), and how vigorously Paul contended against them. But there is enough evidence scattered elsewhere in the New Testament (Acts 20:29-30; Revelation 2:6-7; Ephesians 4:3-6,14) to indicate that the sects began making trouble almost from the start. By the time the Pastoral Epistles appeared the problem was becoming really acute.

23

52 What do the Pastoral Epistles have to say about the sects?

Something of the seriousness of the problem may be judged from the fact that I Timothy launches into the subject of the very first thing (1:3-7). False teachers are spreading doctrines which are upsetting the Church. Then, too, there are those who are stirring up trouble on the subject of the Jewish Law (1:8-11). What the specific doctrines may have been which the heretics taught we do not know, though we do know the names of at least two of the disturbers (1:20). Now and again preachers appeared who taught various absurdities concerning marriage, foods, and personal conduct (4:1-4.) In other cases they simply taught heresies because it was profitable to do so (6:3-10). In still other cases the heretics did render the Christian movement some service.

53 How could a heretic help?

In Colossae, as we have seen, a heresy known as "Gnosticism" made its appearance, to combat which Paul wrote his letter to the Colossians. This heresy taught that there were various divinities, each of a different rank and quality. According to this heresy Jesus was one of the many. By the middle of the second century A.D. this heresy had swept through the Christian Church working considerable damage.

About that time there appeared inside the Christian movement an energetic Greek named Marcion, a wealthy shipowner who made theology a side line. He decided that Christianity was too much under the influence of Hebrew religious ideas and undertook to divorce it entirely from its Jewish heritage and background. Influenced by Gnostic teachings, he declared his belief in two Gods—the Hebrew god Jehovah, and the Christian God. Fearful that the Hebrew Scriptures with their constant reference to Jehovah would unduly influence the Christian movement, he proposed that there should be a body of Christian Scriptures and that the writings of Paul should make up the new book. To the Pauline books he proposed to add one of his own which he called "Antitheses." By all accounts he must have been a strong personality with a considerable following, and, though he did not succeed in his original purpose, he did focus the thought of the Church on the desirability of a New Testament. It can be said with a considerable measure of truth that we owe our New Testament to a heretic; for, following his lead, the Church began assembling its Christian writings.

54 What does this have to do with the Pastoral Epistles?

It is very evident that the author of the letters to Timothy and Titus is endeavoring to defend the Church against such heresies. There is but one God, he declares, and Jesus is his intermediary (I Timothy 2:5-7). The Hebrew Scriptures owe their authority to the fact that God communicated with their ancient writers (II Timothy 3:15-17), as a consequence of which they are to be respected and revered. Perhaps one of the most striking references is one that seems actually to be directed at Marcion's book and Gnosticism.

55 What is that reference?

Marcion had given his book the name "Antitheses," as we have learned, and this Greek name can also be translated "Contradictions." The Greek word *gnosis*, from which the name of Gnosticism is derived, means "knowledge." It is a little startling, when we are acquainted with these facts, to find I Timothy 6:20 saying, "Avoid the godless chatter and contradictions [*antitheses*] of what is falsely called knowledge [*gnosis*]."

56 Why is this so startling?

The vigorous language of the epistle and the strong denial of the Marcionite and Gnostic doctrines suggest that the letters to Timothy may have been written as late as A.D. 125-50, when these heresies were in full flower. If so, then they could not have been written by Paul. These facts are not at all conclusive, but the use of the words "contradictions" and "knowledge" can hardly have been a pure coincidence. The thoughtful student will see, however, that some of the most baffling and interesting problems in the New Testament lie right under the surface of our reading.

57 When were the Pastoral Epistles written?

It is impossible to answer that question until the question of authorship is settled, but we can study the letters themselves with some profit to learn what light they can shed. First Timothy represents Paul as writing the letter from Macedonia or Greece after leaving Ephesus (1:3). Second Timothy declares it is written from prison, evidently in Rome (1:17; 4:21), where Paul believed himself facing death (4:6-18). The letter to Titus represents the Apostle as being at liberty and planning to spend the winter at Nicopolis, where he wants Titus to join him (Titus 3:12). From these references it must be assumed that Titus was written either before the Timothy letters or between them. But it is impossible to fix any exact date for their composition. There are, however, within the text of the Timothy letters some strong words concerning the Scriptures.

58 What do the Timothy letters say about the Scriptures?

It is very apparent that the author is greatly concerned over the question of the authority of the Hebrew Scriptures, these being the only Scriptures the Christians knew anything about at that time. They have a definite place in prayer, the author says (I Timothy 4:5), and should be read at all services of public worship (vs. 13). In Second Timothy a sweeping declaration is made: "All scripture is inspired by God and profitable for teaching, for reproof, for correction, and for training in righteousness" (3:16). Of much more than passing interest is the quotation from another New Testament book.

59 What is that New Testament quotation?

As we shall learn in Study Number Twelve of this series, the four Gospels began making their way into the thinking of the Church and establishing themselves with authority toward the close of the second century. By A.D. 125, however, they were quoted occasionally alongside the Old Testament Scriptures. It is extremely interesting, therefore, to find in I Timothy 5:18 a quotation from Luke (10:7) and one from Deuteronomy (25:4) presented side by side as though they might be of equal authority and both chosen from the Scriptures. Also, in I Timothy 6:13 we find the name of Pontius Pilate mentioned, and this again suggests Luke, for the third evangelist is the only one of the four Gospel writers who gives the procurator's full name

(Acts 4:27; Luke 3:1). These two passages strengthen the belief that the Pastoral Epistles were written late in the history of the apostolic Church.

60 Was heresy the only problem with which Timothy and Titus had to deal?

Some of the most perplexing problems in any organization are those associated with personalities. As in the case in any movement there were those who undertook to turn the new religious movement to the profit of their own personal fortunes. Self-seekers rushed to join the Church in the hope that it might open for them some door of preferment, personal power, or privileged leadership. Some of those early Christians loved to talk, pretended great scholarship, and put on a show of authority; they undertook to build up their own reputations at the expense of the gospel and the Church (I Timothy 1:3-6; 4:1-2, 7). Others taught an unnatural asceticism (I 4:3) or undertook to impose their interpretations of the Jewish Law upon the Gentile converts (I 1:7-10). Against all such the author warned the leaders of the Church, as well as against those who were guilty of grosser sins.

61 Were gross sins a serious problem of the times?

The licentiousness to which Paul made reference in his letter to the Corinthians was not confined to the city of Corinth, but permeated the life of all the world. It was impossible to gather converts from all classes and nationalities without holding the doors open for some who were guilty of gross indecencies and immoralities. There is at least a hint that some such may have created a considerable problem in the infant Church (I 1:9-10; 3:2-13), for the author becomes quite specific when he begins describing the virtues which must be found in officers of the Church.

62 What does he demand of church officers?

Much emphasis is laid in some quarters today on matters of doctrine. "What does he believe?" is the test applied to any who may aspire to leadership. But the author of the Pastoral Epistles gives scant attention to such qualifications. Instead he looks for evidences of good character and blameless conduct. A bishop, for instance, is to be "above reproach." Then follows a long list of qualifications which are to be required—vigilance, sobriety, good manners, courtesy, hospitality, skill as a teacher. He must be mature, patient, uninfluenced by money, and the husband of one wife (I 3:1-7). Similar virtues are required of other officers of the Church, including their wives (I 3:8-13).

63 What about that question of one wife?

Polygamy had practically disappeared among the Jews, but it continued respectable throughout the Roman Empire; and, while it may not have been widely practiced, it carried no moral, social, or legal odium anywhere outside of Palestine. The fact that the author of the epistle mentions it at all suggests the wide difference between the moral standards of the Christians and those which were acceptable among the pagans. It is precisely at the point of the status of women that Christianity varied most markedly from the contemporary life of the Roman Empire.

64 What is said about women in the Pastoral Epistles?

The author reflects much of the thought of his age in his instructions concerning the status of women. They are not to aspire to leadership in the Church but are to be content with such minor responsibilities as may be assigned to them by the men (I 2:9-15), their service being rendered in silence. The modern reader will probably hesitate a bit about applying any such strict regulations to the church women of today. We must not forget, however, that Paul employed Phoebe (Romans 16:1) and Prisca (Romans 16:3) as workers in the early Church and granted high honors to Lydia, his first European convert (Acts 16:14, 40). It appears, then, that women were used in many instances for specific tasks; and, in spite of the strictness of his injunctions, the author of First Timothy sanctions the employment of deaconesses (I 3:11) and official widows (I 5:9) in some limited types of service.

65 Was discipline in the early Church a serious matter?

First Timothy suggests that it was one of the most serious problems with which the leaders were engaged. The advice to Timothy falls under two heads: (1) counsel concerning the personal life and conduct of the minister, and (2) counsel concerning the internal administration of the Church.

66 How is the minister counseled?

He is to think of his life as a sermon in itself. He is to be diligent as a student and guide his people in their thinking. In Second Timothy there is a suggestion that Paul was accustomed to carry a supply of books with him on his travels (4:13). But no amount of learning can substitute for a life under the influence of Christ. Care of the health of the body is a part of good ministering, and all foolish conversation and idle talk is to be avoided (I 4:6-16).

67 What about the discipline to be enforced in the Church?

The private lives of the Christians were of great importance to the Church. If they were not exemplary, the world could not be expected to accept their faith. One gets the impression from First Timothy that the Church inspected the lives of its members rather minutely, a large part of the responsibility for that inspection falling upon the ministers in charge of the congregations (I 5:1-25). Partly to avoid clashes with the empire, Christians were to be law-abiding citizens (I 2:2-3). Women were to dress modestly (I 2:9); servants were to be obedient (I 6:1-2); the rich were to beware of trusting in their riches (I 6:17-18); and the ministers themselves were to proceed about their duties with due caution (I 5:17-25), neither becoming a party to the sins of their people through careless living, nor proceeding unjustly against any man. Nowhere does the author show his genius to better advantage than in the advice he offers to young administrators.

68 What advice does he give them?

His counsel covered four matters: (1) They were to give first attention to the business of teaching; (2) they were to select and train others who would be capable of carrying on the work of instruction; (3) they were to exercise a strict but kindly and just discipline among the members; (4) they were to oversee the organization without doing the work themselves.

69 What about the teaching function?

The Christian faith was something new. Even veteran

Christians had had but little experience in "the way." There was little of historic procedure or experience to guide them. Gentile converts in particular were ignorant of the religious teachings which were a commonplace to the Jews. The things that were almost a part of the air that a Jewish boy breathed from the earliest years of his life had to be taught to the Gentiles after they had become mature adults. The whole way of life had to be reconstructed and an entirely new system of morals developed among the converts.

In addition to those matters which involved little more than simple morals in some instances, there were the great fundamentals of the Christian faith. These included the basic facts concerning the life and teaching of Jesus, and certain conclusions relative to his divinity which were the logical outgrowth of those facts. In the absence of any textbooks on the subject, these matters had to be taught by word of mouth from teacher to pupil, from preacher to convert. Unless the Christian movement were to become a mere amalgam of absurdities and confusion, this work of teaching must be done with scrupulous care. There were a number of capable leaders in the movement—men like Barnabas, Silas, Apollos, Timothy, and Titus—who must assume this responsibility.

70 Was there no written life of Jesus?

It is difficult to answer this question unless we are able to determine the date of the writing of the Pastoral Epistles. If, as seems very probable, they were composed by an admirer of Paul's about A.D. 125, then it seems likely that the four Gospels had all taken form. Careful scholars are of the opinion that by A.D. 65 there was a rudimentary story of Jesus and his work which was being circulated, the core of which was the resurrection story. Details might vary slightly as different individuals told the story, but in the main it can be said that Christians everywhere were probably familiar with the same general facts. Whether the story was yet reduced to writing is very doubtful, though portions were probably in written form. In addition, it is believed that there were collections of sayings of Jesus in circulation, perhaps in written form. No mention is made in any Pauline writing of any written historical record of any kind. The Apostle seems to have depended entirely upon an oral transmission of the basic record.

By A.D. 125, however, the four Gospels had come into existence in written form and were being circulated in the form of one book among the Christian churches. Not only so, but they were rising rapidly in the esteem of Christians everywhere as the authoritative record of the life of Jesus upon which Christian teaching and tradition rested. According to the letters to Timothy and Titus, the young ministers were to instruct the Christians in this oral tradition which was commonly accepted as "the faith." There is no mention of any book of any kind which is to be used as a text. The teachings included (1) certain basic moral principles, (2) the facts concerning the life and sayings of Jesus, (3) some fundamental conclusions concerning the nature and work of Jesus. References to "sound" doctrine and the like appear at least six times in the Pastoral Epistles (I Timothy 1:10; 6:3; II Timothy 1:13; 4:3; Timothy 1:9; 2:1). This indicates that some line was drawn between the "orthodox" and "unorthodox" among the teachings that were current.

71 What about the choice of church leaders and officers?

This seems to have been left largely to the judgment of the great leaders of the Church, and the Pastoral Epistles laid the responsibility squarely on the shoulders of Timothy and Titus. As Paul had chosen his traveling companions and assistants without advice from anyone, so they seem to have inherited the authority to choose leaders for local congregations. So far as any New Testament record goes, the congregations had no voice in this matter. In describing the seriousness of such choices the author of the epistles lays the major emphasis upon the necessity of holy living rather than upon any correctness of doctrinal belief.

72 What was the work of such leaders?

The property interests of the young Church were negligible as yet. So far as we know, no congregation owned a house of worship or other holdings. The only money any church officer handled was such money as might be gathered up to be expended for charitable purposes. The major duties of the church leaders, therefore, were spiritual in nature. They were to instruct the people and train them in the faith. The Church must be guarded from pagan teachings from the outside and from mistaken teachings that came up from inside the membership. A careful distinction had to be drawn between the pretentious learning by which the Greeks set much store and the spiritual and moral truths which were the foundation of the Christian faith.

73 What about discipline in the Church?

Discipline was to be administered for the benefit of the offender and not for the gratification of the vanity, nor to appease the anger, of the minister. Final authority reposed in such leaders as Timothy and Titus, from whose judgments there was no appeal. The infant Church had not yet come to the place where congregational conscience and judgment could be trusted. Just as one can learn much about the civilization of any people by studying the system of punishments meted out to offenders, so we can learn much about the inner life of the Christian church of A.D.75-125 by studying the Pastoral Epistles and noting those offenses which called for disciplinary action.

74 Who were the common offenders?

The epistles mention several groups, among which are (1) those who circulate dangerous teachings, (2) those who neglect kinsfolk who are in need, (3) those who offend the common decencies of life, (4) church officials who betray their trust, (5) those individuals who practice immoralities condemned even by the pagan standards, (6) those who are guilty of excesses of temper and passion whereby the Christian community is brought into disrepute. It will be noted that doctrinal correctness is almost completely ignored and that the major emphasis is laid upon moral uprightness.

75 What were their administrative duties?

Timothy and Titus, being responsible for choosing officials, were also responsible for supervising their activities. Their choices were to be made upon the basis of their Christian character as individual leaders, and their ministers were to be judged on the basis of their usefulness as spiritual guides. This was a period when churchmen were judged by their spiritual and moral maturity and by the superior quality of the lives they lived.

76 What about the letter to Titus?

Very probably it was the second of the three to be written, being preceded by First Timothy and followed by Second Timothy. The same person was doubtless the author of all three, which should in fact be read as one book. It is addressed to the young man Titus, who was, like Timothy, one of Paul's colaborers.

77 Who was Titus?

He was a Christian preacher who seems to have been held in very high esteem by Paul, but, strange to say, his name is never mentioned in the book of Acts. Such fleeting glimpses as we get of him appear only in Paul's letters to the churches. Little or nothing is known of his antecedents, though there is a tradition to the effect that he was born in Crete. Some ancient writings infer that he was living in Iconium at the time of Paul's first visit there, but all we can be sure of is that he was one of the Apostle's converts, that he was a Gentile (Galatians 2:3), that he was living at Antioch when the dispute arose concerning the circumcision of Gentile converts, and that at one time and another he was entrusted with errands of considerable responsibility. He accompanied Paul to Jerusalem following the Antioch council, and there an attempt was made to compel him to undergo the rite of circumcision; but Paul defended his case stoutly, and it was not performed. He was one of those who helped gather in the collection for the Jerusalem saints who were in poverty, being deputized to receive the funds from the Corinthian church (II Corinthians 8:1-6). He was also commissioned to pacify certain elements in the Corinthian church when trouble arose within the congregation on a certain occasion (II Corinthians 12:18; 7:11-15). He seems to have enjoyed the full confidence of Paul and was of very great personal assistance to him on a number of occasions.

78 Why was the letter written to Titus?

He seems to have been put in charge of the church at Crete, and as its chief minister he faced some difficult problems which the letter hoped to help.

79 What was the Cretan church?

So far as the book of Acts goes, we have no record of the

founding of the church at Crete. If Paul ever conducted a missionary campaign there, it must have been at some time following his release from his first Roman imprisonment (if there was such a release). This letter constitutes one of the strongest reasons for believing that Paul was released from his first incarceration in Rome, and that he conducted a second missionary campaign before his final imprisonment and death. This conclusion would be reasonable whether we took the position that Paul wrote the letter or that it was written by another. In either case such a ministry would be necessary to explain the order of events suggested by the letter to Titus.

80 What was the problem of the Cretan church?

The people of Crete had earned a very bad reputation throughout the world as a vagabond, unreliable, untruthful, loose-living lot. Even pagan writers of the time commented on the low moral standards which prevailed on the island, a contemporary poet describing them as "liars always." Titus' problem, then, was to build a self-respecting church of high moral character out of such unpromising material, officer it with godly people, and establish it as a redemptive force in the midst of a dissolute population.

81 Under what circumstances was the letter written?

There is nothing to indicate the place from which the letter may have been written; neither is there anything to suggest what may have been the immediate cause for writing the letter, beyond one or two minor matters. Paul is represented as being in company with Artemas, Tychicus, Zenas, and Apollos—all conspicuous figures in the Christian movement (Titus 3:12-13). These four were expecting to visit Titus in Crete within a short time and may have been entrusted with the delivery of the letter.

82 What was the message to Titus?

The message of the book is quite similar to that of First Timothy. The greeting is an extended one (1:1-4) and somewhat less personal even than that which was extended to Timothy in the first letter (I Timothy 1:1-2), though each is addressed to a "child" of the Apostle. Then follows a series of instructions concerning the choice and organization of church leaders (1:5-9), some counsel regarding the best method of dealing with disturbers who are upsetting the faith of the people (1:10-16), in which the minister is advised to take summary action (1:13). Simple and chaste morals are insisted upon (2:1-15), from which requirement none are exempt. The injunctions are more moral than doctrinal, though a proper belief may have been expected to produce right conduct. The Cretans are exhorted to be law-abiding citizens (3:1-11) who might merit the confidence and respect of the authorities. The letter closes with personal greetings and a word of commendation for two missionaries and two travelers, one of whom is a lawyer (3:13). Apollos, the fourth member of the company, may or may not have been the individual mentioned in the book of Acts (18:24 ff.) and the first letter to the Corinthians (3:6).

83 What is the value of the book?

It should be read along with the two letters to Timothy, and the three should be judged as a unit; for they are all from the same hand, written under the same conditions, and they apply to the same general problems. They are practical rather than doctrinal, administrative rather than devotional, and disciplinary rather than theological. They should be read as earnest counsel offered to young pastors by a wise Christian who is well aware of the stark humanity of the vast majority of the Christians.

84 What about Second Timothy?

This brief letter completes the triology of Pastoral Epistles. It is quite the most exalted of the three and, in some respects, one of the most impressive writings in the New Testament. It seems to have been written from Rome. Paul says that he is alone, except for the companionship of Luke (4:11). The outlook is very bad, the end being in sight (4:6-7). Onesiphorus, an Ephesian Christian, has hunted him up and brought him much cheer in a recent visit (1:16-18) for which he is profoundly grateful.

85 What is the occasion for the book?

It seems that Timothy was expected to visit Paul very shortly, and in anticipation of that event Paul is asking that one or two minor matters be cared for. Some books and a cloak are to be carried to Rome (4:13), but Paul's special concern seems to be in some private papers. Various speculations have been invented to explain what these papers were, but they all end where they begin. We do not know. Yet however simple the occasion for writing may have been, the message of the book is very gripping.

86 What is the message of the book?

A single statement in the book (4:16) suggests that there had been two trials, or that one trial had occurred and another was already impending. This strengthens the argument that he had experienced two imprisonments, having been "rescued" (released) in the first instance (4:17); yet as has been said, there is no historical record remaining to us which throws any light on the situation. We must grope our way, content to study the words of the letter, and take them for what they are worth, leaving some extremely interesting and important questions unanswered. If Paul was not the author of the Pastoral Epistles, then at least we can be sure that there are more statements in Second Timothy which bear the genuine Pauline stamp than in either of the other two, for the book is in every way the most valuable of the three. It may have been that Paul had, from time to time, actually sent letters to the two young preachers containing instructions of one sort and another. It is possible that one situation called for one letter of instructions and another situation called for another letter. These could have been very brief notes dealing with isolated circumstances. In the course of time a number of such came into the possession of some admirer of Paul's and were put into something like their present form, with the best of them collected in Second Timothy, in an effort to make Paul speak to the Christian leaders a generation or more after the Apostle's death.

The letter opens with a gracious greeting to Timothy (II 1:1-2), which is followed by an extended appreciation of the young man who must have been a source of great joy and satisfaction to him through many long years (1:3-14). Paul is perfectly sure that his preaching days are done. With reluctance he assigns the work to Timothy and gives him his final instructions (2:1-13). The great central truths of the gospel are to be kept constantly before the people; contentions are to be discouraged; the gospel will be preached most effectively by an upright life and

36

Christlike conduct (2:14-16). To indulge in idle speculation, no matter how fascinating the theme—even on the resurrection—will inevitably lead to ungodliness (2:16-18). In all things the Christian preacher must set an example of righteous living (2:19-22) and avoid shameless debates and arguments that lead to distemper and irritation (2:23-26). The good minister of Jesus Christ may expect to encounter evil days (3:1-8), and he must count on suffering as one of the certainties of life (3:9-12), but faithfulness will prevail in the end (3:13-14). At this point the author commends the Scriptures (3:15-17) as a constant, reliable, and fruitful source of inspiration and help for the hard-pressed. The last chapter is one of the most moving bits of writing in all the Bible, and surely must have come almost directly from the hand of Paul without alteration. The old campaigner is closing the book of his life. He has no apologies or regrets. His record is clear. His life is about to be offered as a sacrifice for the cause, and the prospect fires him with an exultation of spirit the warmth of which can be felt all the way down through the centuries. It has been a glorious experience; his rewards have been abundant; he awaits death and immortality with a holy eagerness.

87 What happened to Timothy and Titus?

It is impossible to answer this question. There are traditions but no historical records. The Church Fathers make brief mention of them in passing, but there is no dependable testimony upon which we can base any positive assertions. We would like to believe that they kept the trust committed to them by their great father in the faith, and in this we have full warrant. But as the Church grew and the numbers of the Christians increased, it became impossible for any man to keep in touch with the entire movement. The salt was saving the earth, and strong leaders were rising in the East and in the West. The simple organization that sufficed in Jerusalem the year following Pentecost was succeeded by a more elaborate system in which great councils, assemblies, scholars, and ceremonies figured. As the Church grew and congregations multiplied, so the New Testament grew, and upon the foundations laid by faithful men like Timothy and Titus the vast structure of the Church universal was raised.

88 What was the next New Testament book to be written?

Because of the difficulty of determining exact dates in the case of several New Testament books it is impossible to declare with absolute certainty which book followed the Pastoral Epistles, but for the sake of convenience we shall study first the book of James, and in doing so we shall discover that it belongs to this same general period.

89 What is the book of James?

It is the first group of seven books in the New Testament which are commonly known as the "General Epistles."

90 What are those seven books?

James, First and Second Peter, First, Second and Third John, and Jude.

91 Why are they called General Epistles?

Because they were presumed to be addressed to the entire Christian movement. In the case of James, however, the book has had a strange career.

92 What is strange about the book of James?

There was considerable debate in the early Church as to whether or not it should actually be included in the New Testament canon, and the issue was not finally settled until the third council of Carthage in A.D. 397. It was not included in the Muratorian canon (toward the end of the second century), nor was it in the old Latin version which was used by the great scholar Tertullian, about A.D. 200. It was recognized as an authentic member of the canon by Jerome in A.D. 404; Origen quoted from it in A.D. 200; and Eusebius (A.D. 314) listed it as one of the books concerning which there was some dispute. Martin Luther held a very low opinion of the writing and called it "a right strawy epistle."

93 What was the reason for this uncertain record?

There were three reasons: (1) There was considerable

question in the early Church concerning its authenticity as a writing from the pen of one of the Apostles. (2) There was a feeling that its cast of thought was more Jewish than Christian and therefore not entitled to a place in the canon. (3) It was believed to be opposed to Paul's doctrine of salvation by faith.

94 By whom was the book written?

It opens with the simple declaration that is was written by "James, a servant of God and of the Lord Jesus Christ." But then the question immediately arises, "Which James was this?"

95 Were there more than one James?

The name James in the New Testament is the English form of the Hebrew name "Jacob," and four individuals bearing that name are mentioned in the New Testament.

96 Who were those four?

1. There was James the son of Zebedee and the brother of John, who was numbered among the apostles. He was beheaded by Herod in A.D. 44 (Acts 12:2) and could hardly have been the author, for the book bears evidence of having been written very much later than that date.

2. There was James the son of Alphaeus, one of the apostles, who seems to have been known also as "James the younger," the son of Mary (Mark 15:40). Of him we know practically nothing beyond these few simple facts.

3. Then there was James the father of the apostle Judas, not Iscariot (Luke 6:16), about whom nothing is known beyond the mere mention of his name.

4. The fourth James, along with Simon, Joseph, and Judas, was a brother of Jesus (Matthew 13:55; Mark 6:3; Galatians 1:19). His exact identity is veiled in some obscurity. There are those who believe he was the son of Mary and Joseph, in which case he would have been younger than Jesus. Then there are those who believe he may have been a son of Joseph by an earlier marriage, in which case he would have been considerably older. There are still others who believe he was a cousin of Jesus, for the words "brother" and "cousin" are sometimes used rather loosely by the New Testament writers as well as by most writers of that period.

97 Was Jesus' family Christian?

It is well known that Jesus' early ministry caused his family no little concern (Matthew 12:46-50; Mark 3:20-33) and that his brothers at one time did not believe him (John 7:5). Mary, his mother, seems to have been deeply impressed with his powers at the outset of his ministry (John 2:1-12), but she seldom appears during the period of his active ministry, and it is very significant that, when Jesus on the cross was making provision for his mother, he committed her to John, who was in no way related to the family (John 19:26). If he had had the confidence of his blood brothers, it would have seemed natural to expect him to repose the trust in one of them. Following the resurrection Jesus appeared to his brother James (I Corinthians 15:7), and possibly as a result of this visit James became a Christian and immediately joined himself to the little band of Christians (Acts 1:14), together with other members of the family. But there is no record that his family gave Jesus any real support during the period of his earthly ministry. True, his mother is reported as having commended him at the time of the wedding feast at Cana (John 2:5), but on other occasions her visits were not marked by personal endorsements. The fact that Joseph was called a "just man" (Matthew 1:19) indicates that the head of the house was one who observed the Law strictly and ruled a home which was permeated with religious teachings and atmosphere.

98 Which James was the author of the book of James?

There is little or nothing in the book itself which gives us anything more than a slender clue. Both from the name—"James" is the English form of "Jacob"—and from the epistle it may be inferred that the author was a Jew who had been converted to the Christian faith (James 1:1; 2:1; 5:8-9). He was not an apostle, or he would surely have claimed that position. To be such was a great honor and entitled one to make vast claims on his own behalf as a spokesman for the faith. The student will remember that Paul made a vigorous defense of his right to speak as an apostle, and it would seem perfectly reasonable to expect the author of James to make a similar claim if he had been actually a member of the apostolic group. The fact that the book makes no claim to apostolic origin seems to eliminate James the brother of John as the possible author, as well as James the son of Alphaeus. Moreover, as noted above, the former James was beheaded in A.D. 44.

Another James in the New Testament seems to be ruled out—James the father of Judas (not Iscariot). No scholar, so far as we know, makes any such claim for this worthy. This leaves but one other identified James to be considered—James the brother of Jesus.

99 Did Jesus' brother write the book?

There are those who say he did, and there is some reason for the statement. The fact that the author is so well known that he does not need to identify himself would seem to lend credence to that belief. There are, however, other evidences which throw serious doubts upon any claim for his authorship. Certainly the book does not claim any family relationship to Jesus, and some of the doctrines it teaches do not seem to fit into the theory that Jesus' brother is its author, though it is well known that he was the virtual head of the church in Jerusalem (Act 15:13; Galatians 2:9, 12). It will be necessary to examine this question at some length.

100 How had he become head of the Jerusalem church?

The process by which he was chosen is unknown to us. Very evidently he rose to his post by reason of three factors: (1) his close kinship with Jesus must have given him great influence in spite of the fact that he had not been a member of the band of disciples. (2) A leader was needed for the Jerusalem congregation, and the eleven disciples were away from Jerusalem much of the time conducting missionary campaigns. In their absence it would have been natural for the Christians to turn to James for leadership, and in time he would have established himself as the head of the Jerusalem church. (3) It is known that Peter reported to him (Acts 12:17), and one gets the impression that Peter acknowledged the superior position of James, as head of the Church, in doing so. The Roman Catholic Church has always claimed that Peter was the head of the Church, because of his connection with the church at Rome, but the testimony of this early history does not bear out that contention. Paul called upon James soon after his conversion (Galatians 2:9) as if he

41

might have been the responsible head of the movement; the Jewish Christians looked to him as their leader (Galatians 2:12), for he seems to have been something of a stickler for the Law (perhaps a result of Joseph's training), though he did take a generous attitude toward Gentile converts (Acts 15:1-21). Paul visited James a second time, about A.D. 58, in an effort to avoid a clash with the Jewish zealots (Acts 21:18-26) and carried on all negotiations with him to that effect, no one else seeming to have any authority to judge in the matter. What James's final fate may have been we do not know, though Josephus says he was stoned to death about A.D. 62 by the high priest Ananus.

101 Do we know anything definite about the author?

His excellent Greek style and vocabulary mark him as a man of education and culture. He seems to have been a "teacher" among the Christians, and there seems to be a certain correspondence between his teachings and those found in the Sermon on the Mount section of Matthew (Compare James 1:13 with Matthew 6:13, James 4:12 with Matthew 7:1, and James 5:12 with Matthew 5:33-37). The book of James seems to have been a Christian sermon, or a collection of sermonettes, more or less characteristic of Christian preaching of the early part of the second century.

102 What can we decide about the authorship of James?

No question in all the study of the New Testament has aroused greater controversy than that of the authorship of the book of James, and it is impossible to make a conclusive statement about the matter without being confronted by serious questions. About the best we can say is that the book must have been written by a prominent Christian preacher who had the confidence of the Church. His name was James, but concerning his actual identity there is no positive proof. Generally speaking, the weight of evidence seems to swing in favor of some unknown James who wrote early in the second century. Whoever he was, his writing should be studied as a sermon more or less representative of that period.

103 Why call it a sermon?

The book bears no particular title, nor does it reflect a specific historical situation. It is addressed to the "twelve tribes in the dispersion" (1:1), and its message is timeless. The word "dispersion" was used among the Jews to refer to those representatives of the race who were scattered to the far ends of the earth, and this use of the expression in James is highly significant. The Christians regarded themselves as "the real Israel," because they worshiped the Messiah, who had appeared in the person of Jesus. They were, then, the spiritual descendants of the nation and the inheritors of the promises made to Israel. "The twelve tribes in the dispersion" on the lips of James meant the world-wide Christian community. The words in James 1:22 suggest that the people are listening to a sermon, and there is a similarity between the book of James and the ancient diatribes of the Greek orators and rhetoricians which have come down to us.

104   What was a diatribe?

In modern English the word is used to describe a vicious and bitter speech, but among the ancient Greeks it had a meaning somewhat different. True, it was usually strongly flavored with scorn and acidic humor, but it was essentially an informal address on some moral, ethical, or philosophical theme. The Greek world was full of preachers of various creeds, and the Christian preachers adopted their manner and method in very large part.

105   Who were those ancient Greek preachers?

They were a rather numerous class throughout the Greek world. They might preach the doctrines of the Stoics, the Epicureans, or others, but their method was always the same. Equipped with a rough cloak, a begging bowl, and a clever stock of repartee to which was added a substantial bit of solid learning, they would take up their post at some street corner or in a market place amid the crowd and start a conversation with who ever would listen. These conversations (homilia, in Greek, from which we have the word "homiletics," meaning the art of preaching) attracted crowds, and to the people who gathered around, the preacher expounded his doctrines to the best of his ability. When interest was at its height he would pass his begging bowl through the crowd to gather in a few coins which would provide for his living. This was the method Paul followed on Mars Hill (Acts 17:17 ff.) with the exception of the begging-bowl feature. He always prided himself on the fact that he never asked a penny for himself. Some of the more popular and learned lecturers hired halls and charged fees, and Paul was taunted on at least one occasion with the fact that he did not follow that custom. His letters to the churches, however, show very definitely that in his manner of presenting a case he was much influenced by the vogue of the day.

106 What about James in this respect?

It is utterly impossible to reduce the book of James to any orderly outline. In its general form it resembles the late Wisdom Literature of the Jews of the period immediately preceeding the Christian era, consisting of a series of observations strung together without any apparent design. It is dominated, of course, by the Christian emphasis and viewpoint, but it can best be appreciated if we read it as though it is a series of excerpts—either from an extended sermon or from a number of sermons, all by the same author, in which the total message of the preacher is suggested by characteristic quotations.

107 Where was the book of James written?

It is impossible to give a precise answer to this question, for there is nothing in the book that suggests any one locality. Certainly there is nothing in it that hints at Jerusalem, and this has been suggested as one reason for questioning its authorship by James the brother of our Lord. The most that can be said with assurance is that evidently it was written somewhere in the Gentile world by a teacher of the Christian Church.

108 When was it written?

The book bears no date, and any answer we can give must be based on whatever evidence we can find in the book itself. This appears in four forms: (1) its conflict with Paul's theology, (2) its emphasis on the moral conduct of the Christians, (3) the issues with which it deals, (4) its literary style.

109 What about the conflict with Paul?

Paul laid much emphasis on his doctrine of salvation by faith, by which he meant an intellectual acceptance of the claims made in behalf of Jesus, coupled with loyalty to Jesus as the Messiah and a faith in the promises made by Jesus in God's behalf. When Paul said that we are saved by faith, he meant that a Christian would be justified on account of his faith rather than by a keeping of the Law. This doctrine had been perverted by some to mean that so long as one "had faith," it made no difference what his moral conduct might be. The book of James takes issue with this teaching, perhaps because of the perversions which had grown out of it, saying that faith without works is dead, or that it has no value or importance. But in this instance the thing happened which has happened so many times in religious discussions—two people used the same word with entirely different meanings. To Paul "works" meant the observance of the Law as a means to salvation; to James "works" meant the practice of Christian ideals of morality (See James 2:14-26).

110 What does this have to do with the date of the book?

Soon after the turn of the century Paul came to have very great influence throughout the Christian movement. His letters to the churches had been collected and were being circulated as one body of Christian literature, and were molding Christian thought to a very considerable degree. During Paul's lifetime Paul was a formidable antagonist in adebate, but with his passing, and with the rise of perversions of his teachings, someone opposed to his ideas could get a hearing. This argues for a post-Paul date for the book of James.

111 Is there any other reason for accepting a late date?

The first Christians were recruited very largely from among the poor, and Paul's ministry was spent very largely among such workers in the various Greek cities he visited. From among them he won his converts in large numbers. In time, however, more and more people of modest wealth began coming into the movement, and this sometimes resulted in problems of administration within the brotherhood. Luke's Gospel, for instance, was extremely sympathetic with the poor, and in the case of James the author seems to have a violent prejudice against the rich. He writes as though he considered wealth itself as something evil, like lust or gross sinning, to be avoided at all costs (2:6-7; 5:1-6). Such strictures against money and men of wealth would hardly have been necessary or appropriate during the earliest years of the Church, but they would have point at a time when moneyed men were being included in the brotherhood. This seems to be a reason for fixing the date of composition comparatively late.

112 What about the issues with which the book deals?

The author seems to be little concerned with theological questions, such as those which so frequently engaged the attention of Paul. Rather, his interest seems to be in practical issues—the sufferings the Christians face, the importance of a practical faith as contrasted with a faith of mere theory, a decent concern for the welfare of the poor, the dangerous character of sharp speech and ill-temper, and the high value of humility and sincerity. These are virtues of the sort that Paul deals with in his famous twelfth chapter of Romans and his even better known thirteenth chapter of First Corinthians.

113 What about its literary style?

Jesus spoke the dialect of the Palestinian Jews. The first Christians in Jerusalem followed him in this respect. As the gospel spread out into the Gentile world more and more preaching was done in Greek. It is the belief of many scholars that Peter spoke the Palestinian dialect—Aramaic—in Rome and that his sermons were translated into the Greek by Mark, his companion and interpreter. But as the Church grew and the break with the Jerusalem Jews became more and more sharp, the use of Greek became universal. The first Christian writers, if they were Jews, probably wrestled with their Greek as do college freshmen. Paul himself, reared in a Greek city as a boy, used the Greek language, but he never became a good stylist in the use of Greek, some of his sentences being awkward and confused. In the case of James, however, we have one of the most perfect pieces of Greek composition in all the New Testament. In the opinion of many scholars this argues for the proposition that James was written late in the first or early in the second century at least.

114 What can we conclude from all this evidence?

From all the evidence available it seems probable that the book of James was written about A.D. 100, though of course this can be no more than an estimate.

115   What is the character of the book?

There are those who say that the book is not a Christian writing at all but an ancient Hebrew tract which has been appropriated by the Christians. There are others who say very positively that it is Christian of the highest order, both in viewpoint and purpose. Between these two assertions the dispute has raged.

116   Why do they say it is Jewish?

The student should note the fact that the name of Christ appears only twice in the entire book (1:1; 2:1) and then in the most casual manner. Indeed, it is said that it could have been inserted for convenience' sake. Christian doctrines are scarcely mentioned (5:7, 14). Its chief concern is the moral and social conduct of men in general, whether they are Christian or not. Search if you will, and you will find no mention whatever of Pauline doctrines, of the resurrection, of any sayings of Jesus or any references of any kind to his life—though, as has been mentioned (Question No. 101), there is a marked similarity between specific passages and specific words of Jesus. Those who say it is Jewish declare it could have been written by a Jewish teacher of ethics even if Jesus had not lived.

117   Why call it Christian then?

It is a mistake to label men or ideas as being Christian or non-Christian upon the basis of mere words. It makes little difference whether groceries are delivered to our homes in paper or wooden boxes. Our interest is in the groceries, not in the delivery boxes. Now words are only the containers of ideas, and if often happens that the same idea may be packed in several different words. There is something analogous here in the case of the book of James. The author seems to be familiar with the gospel tradition, for we get echoes thereof in a number of passages (compare James 2:5 with Luke 6:20; 2:8 with Mark 12:31; 2:13 with Matthew 6:14-15; 5:9 with Matthew 7:1; 5:12 with Matthew 5:33-37; 5:14 with Mark 6:13; 5:19 with Luke 17:3). The Christian character of the book is not to be determined on the basis of the precise words used but by the ideas themselves.

When we set out from this point of view, we find much in it that is Christian in spirit. True, James is impatient at times of theological hairsplitting and insists upon a practical religion of uprightness (1:27) which is to consist of kindliness and charity as well as of chastity of mind.

118   Is this a sufficient gospel?

It must be admitted that, in spite of the fact that there are many religious gems in the thoughts expressed by James, we do not have a complete system of Christian doctrine or belief. In James's definition of religion pure and undefiled there is a kinship to Micah's word: "What does the Lord require of you but to do justice, and to love kindness, and to walk humbly with your God?" (Micah 6:8). But James fails to see that a vivid moral sense is a product of a deep spiritual conviction. He speaks of a "law of liberty" (1:25; 2:12), but this seems to be no more than a license to act more freely than one could under the old Hebrew Law, a new *power* has been made available, and that this new power creates a new life in which all the virtues by which James sets such high store became a certainty. Because of this lack of spiritual discernment Martin Luther, as we have seen, called the book "strawy."

119   What is the real message of the book then?

We can do no better in replying to this question than to quote from Dr. Edgar J. Goodspeed's *Introduction to the New Testament:*

The trials of life should be received with joy, for they develop character, 1:2-4. A steadfast faith is essential to effectual prayer, 1:5-8. Poverty is no misfortune, 1:9-11. Trial really comes from our desires, not from God; all his gifts are good ones, 1:12-18.

We must open our hearts to the message and not only listen to it but obey it, 1:19-27. There must be no partiality shown to the rich and great, 2:1-13. Faith without works is dead, 2:14-26. What harm the tongue can do! 3:1-12. There must be no bitterness or jealousy in our hearts, 3:13-18. We must have pure hearts and motives, 4:1-10. We must not judge others, 4:11, 12. Pride and self-confidence must be avoided, 4:13-17.

The wicked rich are denounced, 5:1-6. We must have patience like the prophets, 5:7-11. There must be no swearing, 5:12. The power of prayer is great, 5:13-20.[1]

---

[1] P. 291. Used by permission of the publisher, University of Chicago Press.

It is significant that the first collection of Christian writings did not include the book. In fact, the first Christian scholar who gave it any special attention was Origen, who lived and preached during the first half of the third century (185?-254?). Previous to this time it attracted comparatively little attention as a Christian writing. It is very strange that the book nowhere mentions the one doctrine which was the keystone of all Christian doctrine and belief—the resurrection. Paul put this at the very center of his preaching, but James does not so much as mention it.

As an earnest and high-minded discussion of those moral virtues which the Christian faith exalts, and as a discriminating judgment of a practical faith expressed in an upright life, the book of James is inspiring reading. But if the Christian Church had had no other gospel than that which is contained in the book of James, it is doubtful that it would have outlived the third century.

The author's frequent use of the word "wisdom" (1:5; 3:13, 15, 17) and the epigramatic style in which he wrote strongly suggest that he was familiar with the Wisdom Literature of the Jews (Proverbs, The Wisdom of Solomon, Ecclesiasticus, etc.), and those who are familiar with these writings will find many parallels in James. His religious faith bears a strong resemblance to the faith of the writers of Proverbs in one respect at least—he makes one's attitudes toward others the supreme test of the religious life (2:1-12) and warns his readers that a consistent discipleship will attract the wrath of the godless.

Two sayings in James (4:1-10; 5:1-6) remind one very strongly of Isaiah (1:2-17) and Amos (5:10-15, 21-24). In one instance (4:8, 10) we are reminded of Micah's immortal words concerning justice, mercy, and humility (Micah 6:8). All in all it may be said that the book is good gospel but it is not the whole gospel. Certainly it does not compare with the carefully constructed system to be found in the book of Hebrews.

121 What is the book of Hebrews?

It is the book which is beset with more questions than any other writing of the New Testament. To get anything like an adequate understanding of its message we must turn aside for a time to get a glimpse of the church at Rome which may have produced the book of Hebrews.

122 What about the church at Rome?

It was the church located at the capital of the world. The first glimpse we get of it in the New Testament is that given by Paul in his letter to the Romans about A.D. 56. By that time it was a flourishing organization with a fine reputation throughout the entire Christian movement. Who founded the church at Rome is not known. The Roman Catholic Church declares it was no less than Peter, the disciples who denied his Lord, but that doctrine rests upon a foundation of evidence which no Protestant historian can accept. Suffice it to say that in A.D. 56 there was a strong Christian group at the capital which met regularly for worship and was rapidly coming to a position of world leadership in the Christian movement.

123 How did it come to that leadership?

By a perfectly natural process. With the government of the world settled in Rome, with politics and commerce converging on Rome, with authority over the life of the world going out from Rome, it was to be expected that the governing forces of the Christian movement should gravitate to Rome. That was exactly what happened. The original fountain from which Christian influences flowed was Jerusalem, of course. But the Jerusalem church lost its chance to lead the Christian movement when it made two mistakes: (1) It assigned itself to the task of preaching to the Jews and left the cultivation of the Gentile field to Paul and other Hellenistic Jews who were Christians. (2) It set out to require all Christians to become Jews by submitting to Jewish rites before they could become Christians. While it was insisting upon these two points the Christian movement by-passed it.

In A.D. 70 the city of Jerusalem was completely destroyed by the Roman general Titus, and in that awful calamity the Jerusalem church shared with other Jews of the city, though some did escape to the city of Pella before Titus finally closed in. There seems to be a reference to this experience in Matthew (24:15-21). About the same time the Gospel of Mark was written in Rome and circulated as the first complete "life" of Jesus to take form under Christian auspices. Thus, by a series of events unplanned by anyone, the center of gravity of the Christian movement passed over from Jerusalem to Rome.

124 What had been the history of the Roman church?

There is a considerable belief among scholars that the first Christian preaching in Rome was done by Hellenistic Jews who had been witnesses of the events of Pentecost. The stoning of the martyr Stephen scattered the Jews who believed in Jesus, many of whom were Hellenists, and the first Roman congregation might very likely have been organized by some of them. From the fact that there was a strong organization there in A.D. 56, with a reputation that was world wide, it is reasonable to infer that the Roman church was organized very early. About A.D. 60 Paul arrived in the city as a prisoner, and continued to live there in his rented apartment for two years (Acts 28:30). It is unthinkable that he would have been so near the Roman church and not have exercised a very profound influence upon the Roman Christians who had had the benefit of Peter's leadership for some period of years. If it is true that he was freed from his first imprisonment, he must have departed from the city about A.D. 63, and may have been absent from Rome when Nero, in that fateful August of A.D. 64, launched his terrible persecutions referred to in Hebrews (10:32-36), and which have been so vividly described by Tacitus: "First those were seized who confessed that they were Christians. Next on their information, a vast multitude were convicted, not so much on the charge of burning the city, as of hating the human race. And in their deaths they were also made the object of sport, for they were covered with the hides of wild beasts and worried to death by dogs, or nailed to crosses or set fire to and when day declined burned to serve for nocturnal lights. Nero offered his own gardens for the spectacle." The Roman Christians had taken an active part in helping the persecuted Christians (6:10) and in all ways had shown themselves faithful and loyal members of the fellowship. Just when Paul may have returned to Rome for a second imprisonment, if a second there was, is not known, but it must have been sometime after the Neronic persecutions; and it is possible that the inflamed mind of the government made his death a foregone conclusion, as is indicated in the second letter to Timothy (4:6). But between A.D. 64 and the time of the writing of the book of Hebrews a great change had come over the Christian Church generally and the church in Rome in particular.

125 When was the book of Hebrews written?

It will be necessary to go into this matter in greater detail a little later, but at this point we can say that it must have been written about A.D. 90-95, by which time a great weariness had come over the Christian Church.

126 What was the cause of that weariness?

There can be no question but that the first-century Christians believed in an early return of their Lord and a speedy setting up of a visible reign on earth. Paul had taught this doctrine to the Christians in Thessalonica, as appears in his two letters to the Thessalonians, though he makes little reference to the doctrine outside of those two letters and his letters to the Corinthians. Others had taught the doctrine, however; for it was evidently derived from the original disciples, who may have based their belief on words of Jesus which have not been preserved for us. This doctrine of the early return of their Lord had served to buoy up their hopes and strengthen their faith. When persecutions broke in upon them they fell back on that hope, in the belief that if they held true their Lord might come and deliver them from their sufferings and establish his visible Kingdom before their very eyes. Certainly they wanted to be ready to share in its triumph, so they held on in spite of all delays. But it was inevitable that an emotional reaction should set in after such ecstasies as occurred among them in Corinth, and by the years 90-95 a great weariness had settled down over the Christian Church. The Kingdom seemed as far off as ever. There was no visible evidence that it would ever come. A general apathy took possession of the Christian forces everywhere, and especially in Rome. The book of Hebrews was written for the purpose of reviving the faith and stimulating the courage of the second-generation Christians.

127 Why call them second-generation Christians?

Because that was exactly what they were. The first generation of Christians converted at Pentecost had all passed away. So also the converts made during the early years of Paul's missionary labors. It is easy to believe that no Christian in the Roman church in A.D. 95 had heard any of the original apostles in person. But it is also probable that large numbers of the members had been Christians for the most of their lives, and they had heard from their childhood the promise of their Lord's return. Then a great test was laid upon the Church.

128   What was that unusual test?

As far back as the days of Augustus Caesar, who reigned when Jesus was born, Roman emperors had toyed with the idea of demanding worship from their subjects as though they were gods. When the Emperor Domitian came to the throne toward the close of the century, he made a bold bid and ordered every person in the empire to worship him as a divinity, and obedience to this demand became a test of loyalty to the empire. In the case of those peoples who believed in many gods this imposed no problem; it only added one more god to their already large collection. But in the case of the Jews and the Christians it was a very serious matter. They could not obey without denying the validity of their faith. They were in something of the position of the Japanese Christians who, until the end of World War II, were required to pay certain honors to the Japanese emperor. This crisis developed just when the church at Rome had reached the lowest level of its spiritual experience. John the Revelator, writing to the Ephesian Christians about the same time, said to them, "You have given up loving one another as you did at first" (Moffatt's translation of Revelation 2:4b), and this describes the situation in Rome which the book of Hebrews was written to correct.

129   Did the Christians really suffer?

The writer of Hebrews describes his work as a "word of exhortation" (13:22), for it was calculated to strengthen the people and to inspire them to meet their trials with courage. They were made the objects of public scorn and ridicule, many were imprisoned, some had their property confiscated, they were not allowed to buy and sell in the market place (Revelation 18:11), the systematic boycott was applied to them in every possible way, they all risked persecutions of the most varied sort. First Peter, describing conditions, called them a trial of fire

(1:7). The whole added up to a condition that was almost intolerable. In the face of such a condition two things were necessary: (1) the Church must be shaken out of its indifference, and (2) the people must be bolstered up so that they would not collapse under the strain.

130 Was it purely a Roman problem?

By no means. The Domitian persecutions extended to the entire empire, and Christians everywhere were suffering the same indignities. But the case of Rome has been cited because the book of Hebrews seems to have been addressed to the congregation there. No one knows where the book may have been written, for there is nothing within it to indicate. Some scholars think it may have been written by someone in a distant city who was calling upon the church at Rome to maintain the faith for the sake of the entire movement, but that is only a conjecture of course. It is sufficient to know that the situation in Rome was more or less typical, and that a word of encouragement to the Roman Christians would be a message to the Christians everywhere.

131 Who wrote the book of Hebrews?

In the King James Version it is called Paul's letter to the Hebrews, but the name of Paul appears nowhere in the text, and the question of Pauline authorship has been disputed almost from the beginning. Careful students no longer accept the book as having come from the hand of Paul. Various suggestions have been made as to possible authors, among them being the assertion that Prisca, the wife of Aquila, may have written it. There is no word in the New Testament to support such a suggestion, though she was known to be a devout, learned, and forceful woman who must have been a considerable force in the early Church. But linking her name with the book of Hebrews is only an evidence of the wide variety of opinions that have been considered.

132 Why not believe Paul wrote it?

The reasons for believing Paul did not write the book of Hebrews number at least four, each of which is of very great weight: (1) It is entirely different in literary style from anything

54

Paul ever wrote of which we have any exact knowledge. (2) It contains none of the characteristic Pauline ideas and no references to any Pauline writings or experiences. (3) The early Church did not believe Paul wrote it, and Christian scholars as early as the second and third centuries made a wide variety of guesses as to who the author might be. (4) Because of this uncertainty of authorship the book was not received as scripture until A.D. 397. Jerome translated it into the Latin in A.D. 404 as a part of his Vulgate, and thus by only seven years did it escape omission from the canon.

Origen, the great Christian scholar, writing in A.D. 225, said, "Who wrote the Epistle to the Hebrews, God only knows." Tertullian, even earlier, had suggested that Barnabas might have written it, and Origen rather followed him in this idea. Many centuries later Martin Luther suggested that it might have been written by Apollos, who was known to be a learned man, but of whom practically nothing is known from the New Testament (Acts 18:24-28). But even though we do not know the author, we know a good deal about him.

133 What do we know about the author of Hebrews?

At least six things: (1) He was a preacher of the early Church who called his writing a "word of exhortation" (13:22). Chapters three and four constitute an excellent example of an early Christian sermon. (2) He was a man of great literary skill, for his book is the only one in the New Testament which seems to have been written with a deliberate effort to make it a literary work. It is written in rich, forceful Greek and carefully planned for logical and literary effect. (3) The author must have been a man of much learning. (4) The Bible from which he quotes is the Greek Septuagint rather than the Hebrew version—indicating that he was either a Gentile or a Hellenistic Jew. (5) He used a style of interpretation common among scholars of the Alexandrian school under the influence of Philo, the great philosopher. (6) He was devoted to the Christian faith with all the great energies of his mind and heart.

134 Why not credit it to Paul?

The book varies greatly from Paul's literary style, and lacks most of the marks of being a letter. Whereas Paul opened his letters with a personal and affectionate greeting, Hebrews plunges immediately into its theme. At the close of the book there is a reference to Timothy (13:23) followed by, "Those who come from Italy send you greetings" (13:24), but in none of this is there any Pauline proof. From the greeting it can be inferred that it is being written from Rome and that the Roman Christians are saluting the other believers, or it may be inferred that it is being written from some other city to the Romans and that the greeting comes from some Romans who are living in the same town with the writer. The use that Clement made of the book is very suggestive.

135 Who was Clement?

He was one of the early Christian leaders whose name and work are closely associated with the church at Rome. Historians speak of him as one of the great scholars of his time and have given to him the name "Clement of Rome." About the year 95 he wrote a letter to the church at Corinth which, as far as we know, is the first communication the Corinthian church ever had with anyone outside of the New Testament writers. In this letter Clement quotes at some length from the letter to the Hebrews, indicating that the composition was well known to the leaders of the Roman church at that time.

136 What was the book of Hebrews?

Its literary form is that of a public address and also a personal letter. As has been suggested, it does not open as a letter might, but as a speech would. In some sections it sounds as if it had been prepared for delivery to an audience, and it may have been a speech that was intended to be read in services of worship. A few personal remarks were added at the end, which evidently were well understood throughout the Church.

137 Why is the book called a letter "to the Hebrews"?

This is another one of those riddles of which there are so many connected with the book. To get an adequate understanding of the case it is necessary to go through a rather lengthy explanation.

In New Testament times the name "Hebrew" was used to designate a conservative Jew who continued to use the Hebrew language even though he might be living in a land where it was

56

not used. He read his Bible in Hebrew and observed all the strict injunction of the ceremonial law. Contrasted with him was the "Hellenistic Jew," who spoke the language of the land in which he lived and conformed to its life in many small ways. He read the Greek version of the Old Testament (the Septuagint) and kept those ceremonial regulations which were reasonably convenient under the circumstances. There are those who have tried to show that the book of Hebrews was written to a group of Christians recruited from among the "Hebrews," but the evidence is far from convincing.

The book does seem to have been addressed to some special group, however. The author says he has been expecting to pay them a visit (13:19); he praises them for their services to other Christians (6:10-11) and expresses regret on account of their slow growth in Christian faith and graces (5:11-12). Just who these Christians of the special group may have been is not entirely clear, though it is pretty generally agreed that they were at least a part of the congregation of Christians at Rome. Yet even this explanation is not altogether satisfactory.

138 Why not?

Because there is nothing in the book itself which applies to Jewish readers particularly. It contains no reference of any kind to distinctions between Jew and Gentile, a difference which even Christian Jews kept alive inside the Christian community. Even more important is the fact that the writer does not seem to be any too well acquainted with the basic principles of the Jewish religion. He seems to think the center of the Jewish faith was its sacrificial system, whereas actually it was the Jewish Law. For what reason it came to be called "The Letter to the Hebrews" no one knows, though it bears that title in the earliest manuscripts we have.

139 How did the author proceed?

Having in mind the fact of the terrible persecutions which confronted the Church everywhere, and well aware of the low spiritual state of the Christians—at least those in Rome—the author of the book of Hebrews sets out deliberately to bolster up their faith. Almost every chapter contains either an appeal or a warning. They are reminded of the sufferings of Christ and urged to be steadfast as he was steadfast, in order that they may

57

be strengthened through their suffering. Jesus had been schooled by suffering, and they too can achieve righteousness by the same stern routine. But to those who are considering an abandonment of their faith he offers the sharpest kind of warning. It is impossible, he says, to restore those who fall away and crucify the Son of God afresh (6:4-6). "If we sin deliberately after receiving the knowledge of the truth, there no longer remains a sacrifice for sins, but a fearful prospect of judgment" (10:26-27a). The people to whom he is writing are in danger of drifting out of the fellowship (2:1), being far removed from the original Christians (2:3) and having grown restless under petty persecutions (10:33; 12:4). They must be stabilized for the terrible persecutions which are to follow. The promise of the Lord's return no longer thrills them (9:28; 10:35-37). The author is attempting to rekindle the glow that once warmed their hearts and made them a conquering host. Hebrews was written in and for a time of crisis.

140 What is his argument?

He undertakes to make them proud of their religion—to remind them that it is not just another religion among all the faiths of mankind, but that Christianity is the only true faith and, as such, the only basis upon which they can possibly build any confidence in God or themselves. This he does by the use of three contrasting propositions.

141 What is the first contrast?

It was the belief of the Jews that their Law had come to them largely by miraculous means through the medium of angels. The author of Hebrews undertakes to show the Christians that Christ is superior to any angels and is to be worshiped instead of angels (chapters 1 and 2). This is reminiscent of the Gnostic heresy.

142 What is the second contrast?

The great figure in Hebrew religion was Moses who had led the people through the wilderness and who had introduced the people to the Law. But Christ, says the author of Hebrews, is a greater figure than Moses and supplants him as God's messenger (chapters 3 and 4).

143 What is the third contrast?

The Book of the Law, in Ezra's time, had come to the people through the labors of the scribes and Levitical priests. But Christ is also superior to them, and as such has a prior claim on the loyalty and devotion of the Christians (chapters 5 to 10).

144 What is his conclusion?

Inasmuch as the Christian's faith is superior to that of the Jews, it is reasonable to expect that the Christians will give to Christ a superior type of loyalty, for their obligations are correspondingly greater (chapters 11 and 12). If the great ones before Christ could live by faith, then those who have known Christ should have an even greater faith (chapter 11). If obedience to the Jewish Law was profitable, then obedience to the Christian way is infinitely more so (chapter 12).

145 What about the argument?

In order to appreciate the book of Hebrews it is necessary to understand the viewpoint of the author, and as we make such a study we immediately discover one of the reasons why it is highly improbable that Paul was its author. A strict "Hebrew of the Hebrews" such as he was would have had a much more accurate understanding of the Jewish faith than the author of Hebrews reveals. According to the writer's interpretation of the Hebrew religion, everything headed up in the high priest. As a matter of fact it headed up in the Law. But the writer of Hebrews largely ignores the Law and builds his argument on the theory that the priestly system is the essential feature of their religious system.

Once every year the high priest went into the holy of holies of the Temple to offer a sacrifice for the sins of the people. There he stood in the presence of God to plead for the people. For that brief space of time he was the personification of the race. In the solemn service in the wilderness a covenant was sealed whereby God became Israel's God, and each year the entrance of the high priest into the innermost sanctuary of the Temple signified the renewal of the covenant.

From this concept of the office of the high priest the author of Hebrews drew a picture of the function and service of Christ. Jesus, like the high priest, was one of the people, and yet he stood in a peculiar relationship to God (5:1ff.). In addition, he had offered himself as a perpetual sacrifice for the sins of the people (9:11-14). Instead of entering for a short time into the presence of God, he had entered permanently into the divine company and remains always at the right hand of God to plead the case of humanity (8:1-2).

It is a little difficult for modern readers to feel the significance of this argument, for we have never lived through the experience of seeing the high priest go into the holy of holies on our behalf. The centuries of spiritual freedom we have enjoyed under Christian preaching have emancipated us from the concept, but, in spite of all that, the book of Hebrews does offer a sublime Christian idea of very practical value.

146 What is the great contribution of the book?

According to the Alexandrian philosopher Philo (a Jew by birth who was learned in Greek philosophy), everything in this material world is but a reflection of something more eternal and real in the spiritual world. This idea was picked up in various forms by various Christians and carried over into the Christian system. The author of Hebrews takes the position that Christ has put us in touch with all needful spiritual realities. By his priesthood he has opened up to every believer the way to God.

To Paul the idea of faith was very definite and clear. It was that attitude of trust and surrender which opens our hearts to the incoming of the Spirit of God. To the author of Hebrews the idea of faith is slightly different. He thinks of it as a power which enables us to sense things beyond the senses. "Now faith is the assurance of things hoped for, the conviction of things not seen," he says (11:1). In proof of this he offers a list of Hebrew heroes who, by exercising faith, have triumphed. They believed in truths which seemed to be contradicted by the facts, and yet these truths triumphed. Of course Christ was the greatest example of all, "who for the joy that was set before him endured the cross, despising the shame, and is seated at the right hand of the throne of God" (12:2), as proof of the fact that crosses, shame, and evil are all doomed. The magnificence of this idea lay in the fact that, whereas in the Old Testament it was only the occasional individual who might have such faith, under Christ *any man might think of himself as the heir of the promise.*

147 How was the book of Hebrews used?

Prepared as it was, as an address to the churches, it seems to have been circulated among the churches for reading in their public meetings. It was a combination of letter and sermon and, while it was addressed to the church of Rome, it was adaptable to any church. It did, however, call upon the Roman church to assume the role of teacher of other churches.

148 Why should the Roman church become a teacher?

Hardly a dozen years after the formation of the first Roman church, persecution broke out under the Emperor Nero, and the Christians suffered terribly. In that awful August of A.D. 64 they learned what it meant to have life swept out from under them and to be brought to the very verge of ruin. But the hope of Christ's return nerved them for the ordeal and within a few years they had recovered. Then came the Domitian persecutions and even more tragic suffering, this time extending all over the empire, and in the midst of the awful days the churches everywhere looked to the church at Rome for leadership. But there was no great leader among the Roman Christians to point the way. Then came the years that followed, and the Church had grown very weary. Many began to think that perhaps Christianity had played out, and again the world looked to the Roman congregation for leadership. The book of Hebrews is a voicing of that expectation. The Christians at Rome ought to be teaching the rest of the Church, the author says (5:12), and this is exactly what happened.

149 How did they teach the church?

We are not quite ready to make a detailed answer to that question beyond the statement that two books were produced by the church at Rome shortly after the book of Hebrews appeared, both of which aimed to do exactly that thing. First Clement, written about 95-96, was addressed to the Corinthian church, and though it never became a part of the New Testament it did exercise much influence and was full of the flavor characteristic of New Testament Scriptures. Then First Peter appeared with this specific purpose written into its very structure. Sometime after A.D. 100 a third book was written by someone inside the church at Rome, being known by the title

"The Shepherd of Hermas," the purpose of which was to modify the doctrine taught in Hebrews that there could be no forgiveness of sin in the case of sins committed after baptism (Hebrews 6:4-6). Ignatius, a Church Father writing about A.D. 110, said in a letter to the Romans, "You have taught others," thus indicating that the Roman church did rise to the role of teacher in the Christian movement.

150 What is the modern value of Hebrews?

The student can be forgiven for asking why a book like Hebrews should claim attention from modern Christians. Aside from the thrilling eleventh chapter it is a difficult book to read. The general text seems to be far removed from modern problems. But if we can see the framework of the text, it may help.

151 Where can such a sketch be had?

Professor H. T. Andrews of London has provided one in *The Abingdon Bible Commentary,* which is offered herewith:

Two main lines of thought in the Epistle—the practical and the intellectual—are so interwoven that it is not easy to disentangle them. The march of the argument is often side-tracked by the digressions. The practical interests of the writer and his earnest moral appeals often override and obscure the elucidation of his theological thesis. It is therefore necessary for the student to study carefully the map of the plan of the book. It we omit the digressions and the paragraphs of practical appeal, it will be found that the development of the line of argument proceeds along the following course: (1) The writer begins in 1:1-14 by proving the supremacy of Christ over the Angels. (2) After a digression in ch. 2 he demonstrates in a short paragraph, 3:1-6, the superiority of Christ to Moses. (3) Then after a long digression in the latter part of ch. 3 and ch. 4 he indicates in 5:1-10 the defects of the priestly system of Judaism and suggests that Christ is the supreme High Priest after the order of Melchizedek. (4) More digressions follow, and it is only when we come to ch. 7 that the line of thought adumbrated in 5:1-10 is worked out in detail and the supremacy of the high-priestly work of Christ demonstrated. (5) In ch. 8 the writer shows that Christ is not only the ideal High Priest but that he ministers in an ideal sanctuary, and his ministry constitutes the establishment of a new covenant between man and God. (6) In ch. 9 the writer demonstrates that Christ as the supreme High Priest offered the supreme sacrifice for the sins of the world. (7) The argument culminates in ch. 10:1-18, where the writer again demonstrates the futility of the Jewish sacrifices, and the finality and completeness of the redemption wrought by Christ. Thus the main argument of the book is found in the following passages; 1:1-14; 3:1-6; 5:1-10; 7:1-10:18. It is in the last section, 7:1-10:18, that the largest and most sustained and most subtle piece of reasoning in the Epistle is found.

The chief digressions from the main argument may be summarized as follows: (1) In ch. 2 the writer turns aside to discuss the significance of the sufferings of Christ. (2) From 3:7 to 4:16 there is a long digression on the promise of rest—a promise which has never yet been realized—and which, therefore, is a great inheritance into which the writer summons the Christians of his own time to enter. (3) From 5:11 to 6:20 there is a long warning against relapse, in which the writer describes the supreme peril involved in forsaking the faith. (4) 10:18-39 contains another great appeal and a further warning of the fate which awaits those who fall away from the Christian faith. (5) Chs. 11 and 12 contain a final challenge based on the heroic story of the saints and martyrs of the past, a further discussion of the meaning of suffering (12:7-13), and a very powerful description of the contrast between the Old Covenant and the New. (6) Ch. 13 gives some final injunction and personal messages.

152 Which New Testament book was written next?

There is some doubt as to exact order in which the books were produced, but we shall not be far off if we next take up the study of First Peter.

153 When was First Peter written?

There is considerable disagreement among scholars on this subject, some believing that the little book was written by the Apostle Peter toward the close of his life during the Neronic persecutions of A.D. 64, and others believing it was written by another during the Domitian persecutions a generation later (93-96).

154   What date seems the more probable?

There seem to be good reasons for accepting the later date: (1) The Neronic persecutions were purely local, while the Domitian persecutions affected the whole world. The book is addressed to Christians in Asia Minor (1:1, 7) who are suffering in a large way. (2) The book is written in exquisite Greek—which could hardly have been expected of Peter, though he might have employed a secretary. We shall proceed however, as though the book were written about A.D. 95, for there is one more reason of still greater significance. (3) The author of Hebrews charged the Roman church with the responsibility of teaching other Christians the essential meaning of the faith (Hebrews 5:12), and First Peter seems to have been a response to this challenge.

155   What was the occasion for writing the book?

The sufferings through which the Christians were passing and the publication of the book of Revelation.

156   What about the persecutions?

Reference has already been made to the Emperor Domitian and his demand that he should be worshiped as a god. Throughout the world the Christians were in trouble just because they were Christians (1:6; 2:12, 20; 3:14,15, 17; 4:12-19; 5:9). Paul had tried to avoid clashes with the empire by urging the Christians to obey the law (Romans 13:1-7); but there was something so basically different between the state and the church that it was impossible forever to avoid a clash, and by the close of the first century, as we learned in connection with the Letter to the Hebrews, the situation was acute.

157   What effect was the persecution having?

Two extremely interesting historical records throw light on the situation. (1) We have a letter from a governor of one of the provinces addressed to the emperor in which he describes the way he is handling the situation in his district. From this letter it is very evident that great pressure was being brought to bear upon the Christians to induce them to recant, and it appears that many did so. (2) In recent years many papyrus sheets have been found which are called *libelli* and which carry affidavits to the effect that the people whose names are signed to the documents were not worshipers of Jesus. These are probably repudiations of the faith signed by fainthearted Christians who were broken under the persecutor's heel.

158 What did Revelation have to do with it?

The book of Revelation, written by a Christian preacher named John, declared that it had been written at the instigation of Christ himself. But some of the statements sound very strange on the lips of one who hung upon the cross and prayed, "Father, forgive them." For instance, "Pay her back in her own coin, and give her double for what she has done. In the cup she mixed for others, mix her a double draught.·. . . . Gloat over her, heaven! and all you people of God, apostles, and prophets, for God has avenged you upon her!" (Rev. 18:6, 20—Goodspeed). This is bitter language and calculated to stir up the spirit of hate among the Christians. At best it must be admitted that it is inflammatory, and, as we shall see when we come to a closer study of Revelation, the entire book is calculated to do that very thing. After a careful reading of First Peter it is easy to believe the book might have been put out as an antidote, and as part of an effort to prevent the Christian religion from becoming a system of mere hatred and vengeance.

159 Where was First Peter written?

It is plainly stated that the book is a product of the church at Babylon (5:13). The ancient city of Babylon was still a considerable metropolis in the first century and contained a considerable number of Jews, though there is no record of any Christian church there. Then there was a Roman military city in Egypt, near the present site of Cairo, which also bore the name Babylon. Neither is there any satisfactory record of any Christian church there. In Revelation the name Babylon is applied to Rome (Revelation 14:8), and practically all scholars believe that the reference in First Peter is borrowed from Revelation, and that raises an interesting question.

160 What point does the name Babylon raise?

The fact that the name was used in Revelation and also in First Peter suggests that the author of the latter was familiar with the former, and that strengthens the inference that First Peter is an antidote for Revelation.

161 How important was this?

The Church faced a critical situation. Persecutions were inflaming the minds of the Christians, and Revelation claimed to speak the mind of Christ. If such a book were accepted it was entirely possible that the Christian movement might become a cult of revolution and be crushed under the heel of the state as an opposition party rather than as a religious faith, and the Church certainly was not strong enough to resist the state.

162 Why is the name Peter attached to the book?

If it were written about A.D. 64 as some think, it would have been possible for Peter still to be alive and compose the book, though there is at least one good reason to doubt Petrine authorship. Paul seems to have influenced the book in numerous places, and it is doubtful if Paul would have influenced Peter very much. The opening sentence, for instance, is a direct quotation from Paul (compare I Peter 1:3 with II Corinthians 1:3 and Ephesians 1:3). The classes with which Peter deals are markedly similar to those with which Paul is concerned (compare I Peter 2:18–3:7 with Ephesians 5:22–6:9). Then there are similarities of ideas, such as loyalty to the state (compare I Peter 2:12-16 with Romans 13:1-7). We know, however, that there was no intimacy between Peter and Paul, and it is unlikely that Peter would thus borrow from Paul. It is believed, therefore, that the name of Peter is attached to the book because the writing is the product of the Roman church.

163 What would that have to do with it?

Mark's Gospel, produced some twenty-five years earlier, was commonly accepted as the gist of Peter's preaching in Rome, and was credited to Mark, his secretary (I Peter 5:13). It was an accepted custom of the time that a church like the one in Rome, intimately associated with one like Peter, should be recognized as his spokesman. Whatever the Roman church said carried the weight of Peter's authority. When the Roman church was challenged to teach the Christian world, what could have been more natural than that they should have appropriated the name of Peter as their authority?

164 Was Revelation widely known?

Concerning the popularity of the book of Revelation there can be little doubt. Because it was written by "John of Ephesus," it seems to have exercised great influence in Pontus, Galatia, Cappadocia, Asia, and Bithynia—provinces which composed the northern half of Asia Minor and which are specifically mentioned in I Peter (1:1). The city of Ephesus was one of the great Christian centers and may be said to have dominated the thinking of the Church throughout all that section of the world. A book that was well received in Ephesus would be very apt to be similarly accepted in the region that was spiritually dependent upon that center.

165 Was First Peter written for these Christians?

The book is addressed "to the exiles of the dispersion in," or (King James Version) "to the strangers scattered throughout" these provinces (1:1). In other words, First Peter is addressed to the churches in the very region where Revelation was most popular.

166 What effect did First Peter have?

It is impossible to point out exact results, for there are no records, but two things can be stated: (1) The Christians did survive the Domitian persecutions, and (2) First Peter has been preserved for us in the New Testament. When it came to making up the canon, this epistle took its place almost without dispute. Perhaps the prevailing idea that any church which had witnessed a saint's martyrdom was at liberty to speak thereafter in his name gave Rome the authority to attach Peter's name to this book.

167 What is the value of First Peter to modern Christians?

In it we have one of the noblest expressions of Christian confidence in all the New Testament. Its portrayal of the Christian life is as lofty as anything we have in the Scriptures. In advising patience and forgiveness in the midst of persecution it has set a standard for Christians of all time. Nothing could have been more mistaken than for the Church to have adopted the policy of revenge suggested by Revelation, and First Peter is an excellent antidote for all that sort of thinking.

168 What is the message of First Peter?

(1) The hope that has come to the Christians through Christ and their responsibility for living in a manner worthy of that blessing (1:1–2:10); (2) advice and counsel, with an exhortation to patience (2:11–4:6); (3) exhortations that have to do with a personal religious experience, together with a plea for patience under persecution (4:7–5:14).

169 Is there no theology in the epistle?

There is but one new doctrine in the book. Twice reference is made (3:18-20; 4:6) to the belief that Jesus descended to the world of the dead and preached there to imprisoned spirits. This is reflected in that phrase of the Apostles' Creed which asserts that Jesus "descended into hell." All who hold to the idea that Jesus went to preach to the dead who had never heard him base their doctrine on these two passages.

170 What is the message of the first division?

The basic theme of the book is hope. At the very beginning of the epistle Christianity is described as a "living hope," and the idea is repeated several times. Sufferers are pointed forward to a better day when wrongs will be made right through this hope. What faith was to Paul, hope is to the author of First Peter. The Epistle opens with greetings to the Asian Christians (1:1-2), and follows with thanks to God for the blessing inherited through Jesus. Trouble is but temporary, and the triumph soon follows (1:3-12). As the Christian keeps his mind on high levels and obeys the commands of Christ, remembering his sacrificing for us, so shall he triumph as Christ triumphed (1:13-25). We must remember that we are to live a superior kind of life, that we have been born to it, that to grow is our duty, for we have a holy destiny to perform, having been called out of darkness into light (2:1-10).

171 What about the message of the second division?

Persecutions will come, but when they do come then Christ is our example, and the Christian's life must honor him in all things, for he died that we might live (2:11-25). Husbands and wives are to live together in peace; sympathy, good will, and clean speech are to be the marks of a Christian (3:1-12). Live uprightly and keep a clear conscience, and if you suffer, let it be for doing right and not for doing wrong (3:13-17). This was the way Jesus lived, and he triumphed (3:18-22). It is not easy to shake off old habits of dissipation but it must be done (4:1-6).

172 What about the third division of Peter?

The end is not far away. Take time to pray, keep your spirit of love, serve one another in Christian grace (4:7-11). Do not be surprised that you are compelled to meet trials of fire, for suffering glorifies a Christian (4:12-19). Put your worries into the hands of God (5:1-11) and he will perfect you. Then follows the simple statement that the letter has been written by Silvanus.

173 Who was Silvanus?

It is impossible to determine his exact identity (5:12). He may have been a Christian scribe who did the writing, or he may have been one of the Christian brotherhood who assisted with the composition of the epistle. One of Paul's companions in his missionary expeditions through Asia Minor and Greece was names Silvanus, or Silas (Acts 15:22–18:5; II Corinthians 1:19; I Thessalonians 1:1; II Thessalonians 1:1), but we cannot be sure he is the one referred to here. The name is a common one and, like the name of James, may have belonged to several devout Christians of the early Church. Much more important is the reference to the "elders" of the Church.

174 Who were the elders of the Church?

The first time we meet an elder as an officer of the Church is in Acts 11:30 and 14:23. Nowhere does Paul use the word. The Christian pastor has become by this time an officer of the Church with perhaps a small salary paid him for his services. The author of First Peter speaks of himself as a "fellow elder" (5:1), which would have been a strange term for Peter to use if he actually wrote the book. It is in connection with this work of the elders that First Clement was written. The church in Corinth was not showing the proper respect for the elder, and Clement wrote some straight counsel on the subject. First Peter likewise calls for respect for the office, indicating that it was just coming into some position of dignity. This is additional evidence that the book must have been written late rather than early in the first century.

175 Did Peter write any other book?

There is another book which bears the name of Peter—Second Peter—concerning which some questions are raised, as in the case of First Peter. Because Second Peter is so closely linked with the book of Jude, and because scholars generally believe that Jude was written first, we shall study it before we turn to Second Peter.

176 What is the book of Jude?

It is a tiny little book of only twenty-five verses which is sometimes lost sight of because it is tucked in between the letters of John and Revelation the last of the New Testament. Its brevity, however, is no index to its interest.

177 Who wrote the book of Jude?

The name Jude is a form of the name Judas, which was a very common name among the Jews of Jesus' time. At least seven different individuals by that name appear in the New Testament. (1) There was Judas who was one of Joseph's ancestors (Luke 3:30), (2) Judas who was one of Jesus's brothers (Matthew 13:55; Mark 6:3), (3) Judas Iscariot (Mark 3:19; 14:10, 43; Acts 1:16, 25), (4) Judas the son of James, and one of the apostles (Luke 6:16; Acts 1:13), (5) Judas of Galilee (Acts 5:36-37), (6) Judas with whom Saul was housed (Acts 9:11), (7) Judas, surnamed Barsabbas, who was one of Paul's companions (Acts 15:22-33. But the author of this little book seems to have been none of these.

178 What does the book itself say?

It says that it was written by Jude the brother of James (1:1); but this does not help much, for the name James is as common as the name Jude. If he had been referring to James the brother of Jesus and the head of the Jerusalem church, that would have made him a brother of Jesus. In that case it seems that it would have been reasonable for him to have called himself "the brother of Jesus." That would have been a far greater distinction and a much more positive identification. The most that we can say in the matter is that the author must have been a Christian who had a brother named James, who, though unknown to us, was well enough known in that day to prove an identification for the author. But in the case of Jude it is not necessary to understand who James or Jude may have been in order to understand the message of the book.

179 When was the book written?

The Book of Jude was written for the purpose of arming the Christian Church against the libertine sects which were developing in considerable numbers during the middle of the second century. It is impossible to fix the exact date of the composition of Jude, but about A.D. 150 seems to be approximately correct.

180 What were the libertine sects?

The Christian religion from the first called itself a religion of the Spirit. It taught that all men had access to the Spirit of God, and that to each individual the Holy Spirit communicated his desires, preferences, plans, and inspirations. Among the Jews it was believed that the Spirit of God communicated with the high priest on specified occasions, as when he entered the holy of holies, and that in times past he had communicated with the prophets, who, in turn, had made those communications known to the people in the form of prophecies and sermons. Between the Christian and the Jewish beliefs there was this difference; The Jews believed God communicated only with chosen individuals on rare occasions, while the Christians believed that every "believer" was the recipient of such communications as a frequent and recurring experience.

This doctrine of the Holy Spirit was appropriated by certain groups and perverted into an extremely dangerous thesis. Divine sanction was claimed for outrageous conduct, it being asserted that the evildoers had received inward communications authorizing their scandalous actions. Thus the approval of God was claimed for lives that were utterly devoid of all moral scruples. Nothing is worse than evil arrayed in the disguise of

71

holiness, and the dreadful heresy began to make serious inroads on the Christian forces.

181 Why were they called "libertine sects"?

Because of the general immorality which characterized them. Paul had taught that the Christian lived under the guidance of the Holy Spirit (Galatians 5:16; Romans 8:1-14) and that he could be trusted to furnish directions for life. Many converts from the pagan religions had lived gross lives as pagans, and it was easy to seize upon this doctrine as a justification for the continuance of their immorality. The name "libertine sects" was not applied to them by their contemporaries, but is a name that has been given them by modern scholars.

182 Was the matter really serious?

Very serious indeed. Our study of Corinthians revealed the low state of morals in Corinth (I Corinthians 6:9-11), and some discussion of morality appears in many of Paul's letters. The Greek standard of personal morality was entirely different from that of the Jew, to say nothing of that of the Christian, though the Jew had been the most chaste and moral individual in the world of that day. A Greek who became a Jew was under the necessity of measuring up to a moral standard he had never before attempted. But if he became a Christian the requirements were much more exacting. Paul recognized the gulf between the two concepts of life and preached the doctrine that Christ made a new creature out of a man (Galatians 6:15, II Corinthians 5:17). Converts who found it difficult to measure up to Christian standards began to excuse their failures by claiming the authority of the Spirit for their acts. Once a man had made such a claim it was difficult to condemn his actions.

183 Why were they called sects?

At first it was only a problem of an occasional individual, but in time such individuals sought each other out and formed groups. Then they claimed to have superior knowledge of the Holy Spirit and proceeded to live above the law. The book of Jude gives us a general idea of the nature of these sects, which must have become a very real threat to the Christian movement.

184 How does Jude portray them?

It is evident that the libertine sects were somewhat similar to the Gnostic sects which were conspicuous toward the close of the second century. (1) They believed they had special communications from God expressed in mysterious language (v. 16). (2) They divided all men into two classes—the "material" and the "spiritual" (v. 19)—classifying themselves as the spiritually minded ones. (3) They taught that there were different gods, that the true God was different from the Creator of the world, and that Jesus was only a man who had some special union with the divine during the time of his ministry (v. 4). Their immorality was the direct result of this loose thinking.

185 Does this provide any hint as to authorship?

The general nature of the material in Jude convinces most scholars that it could not have been written by a brother of Jesus for four reasons: (1) The description of the heretics follows very closely after that found in the Pastoral Epistles, which we have discovered were written too late for any brother of Jesus to have been their author. (2) "The apostles of our Lord" are mentioned in Jude as though they were men of a former age (vv. 17, 18) who had foretold what was actually happening at the time the book of Jude was being written. (3) The faith is spoken of as if it were an established matter of some years' standing. (4) The type of heresy described is known to have come into existence long after the time of the apostles.

186 Did Jude write to the sects?

On the contrary, he wrote to the Christians, "those who are called, beloved in God the Father and kept for Jesus Christ" (v. 1). By this is meant all the Christians who are attempting to maintain their faith and keep their loyalty unimpaired. The letter is not addressed to any one church but is intended as a little "tract for the times" to be read by all Christians.

187 What is its message?

It pleads with the Christians to hold fast to the accepted beliefs of the Church and not to go off after strange doctrines or teachers who deny the true God and Jesus Christ his only Son (v. 4). The divine judgment, he believes, is absolutely certain

(vv. 5-11), and the troublemakers are certainly wicked (vv. 12-18). True disciples will follow the counsel of the apostles and continue steadfast (vv. 19-23). In his concept of Scripture we get one of the most interesting sidelights on the book of Jude.

188 What is the teaching concerning Scripture?

The author quotes with complete confidence from the Book of Enoch and the Assumption of Moses (vv. 6, 9, 14) as though they were Scripture of equal authority with any other books of the Old Testament. These were religious writings which were popular among the Christians of the second century, though they were not accepted by the Jews. Jude's use of them shows that the Christians were beginning to think with some independence on the subject of Scripture, and this was one of the first steps in the direction of the New Testament.

189 What is the value of the book of Jude?

The heresies which it was intended to combat have passed away, so far as their organized forces are concerned. The arguments against them have lost their meaning, except as they condemn immorality in general. Seldom indeed will a modern Christian turn to them in this day, and very little of guidance or spiritual inspiration is to be found within the book, though there is one passage that is as sublime and beautiful as anything in the New Testament.

190 What is that great passage?

It is the noble benediction with which the epistle closes: "Now unto him that is able to keep you from falling, and to present you faultless before the presence of his glory with exceeding joy, to the only wise God our Saviour, be glory and majesty, dominion and power, both now and ever. Amen." (King James Version.) The author says that he had expected to write a longer letter (v. 3) which would have been a broader treatise of the Christian gospel, and one wishes he might have done so. Instead he hastily put his little tract together and sent it out in the hope that it might help to stem the tide of immorality which was inundating the Church. The larger work, however, was attempted by another author, whose work bears the name of Second Peter.

191 Did Peter write this epistle?

In spite of the fact that it carries the name of Peter and that it claims to be from the hand of the Apostle (1:1), competent scholars do not believe he had anything to do with it.

192 What are their reasons?

1. There are historical allusions in the book which do not fit into the period during which Peter was alive and preaching.

2. The little book is never mentioned by any writer until about A.D. 200—which would be very strange if Peter had actually written it and if it had been known to the Church during the first century.

3. There was a literary custom of the time, as had been said, which made it legitimate for another person to use Peter's name. This appears to have happened in this case.

193 What was that literary custom?

It has been referred to a number of times in these studies—the custom of ascribing a book to some famous person, even though he had nothing to do with its actual composition. If the writer believed it was worthy of the person whose name it was to bear, it was considered perfectly honorable to credit it to him. This was commonly practiced in the second century by writers other than those represented in the New Testament, and our scriptural writers simply followed a popular custom.

194 Were there any others that used Peter's name?

Rather curiously, we have several writings of about this same period which used Peter's name. There was, for instance, an Apocalypse of Peter, a Preaching of Peter, Letters of Peter, Revelation of Peter, and a Gospel of Peter—all of which were well known among the Christians and which were even considered by some as being worthy of a place in the New Testament alongside the letters of Paul and the four Gospels. The original authors were making no effort to deceive, and no one thought of their writings, in that day, as forgeries or efforts at deception. They were efforts to get a hearing for ideas which the authors believed were in harmony with the known teachings of Peter.

195   Was Second Peter such a book?

Most scholars believe it was. This is partly proved by the fact that even the ancient Church seriously doubted its Peterine authorship. Some Eastern churches did not recognize it as having come from the hand of Peter, or as being scripture, and some scholars believe today that the New Testament would not have suffered any great loss if it had failed to be included in the canon.

196   Why do they feel so about it?

It has perhaps the least spiritual value of any New Testament book, and in addition a very large part of it is taken bodily from the book of Jude. It is true that direct references are made in it to events in the life of Jesus (1:14, 17, 18) as if the author had been an eyewitness. Paul is alluded to as his "beloved brother" (3:15), and mention is made of the previous epistle (3:1), but all this is believed to be a part of the author's device. Certainly it does not provide us with any new or additional information. None of the Church Fathers recognized the book as having scriptural value until Origen (185?–254?) gave it some attention.

197   What is the purpose of the book?

The doctrine of the second coming of Jesus, which had done so much to maintain the faith of the early Church, was beginning to lose its appeal toward the close of the second century. There were those who were beginning openly to scoff at the suggestion of a second appearance of Jesus (II Peter 3:4). It was to meet this situation and to combat the popular immorality that the little book was written.

198   What is its message?

The three chapters can be said to represent the three major divisions of the book. (1) The readers are urged to hold true to their ancient faith. (2) As in Jude, which is largely incorporated into the second chapter, there is an appeal that the heretics shall not lead them astray. (3) The third chapter makes a stout declaration that the return of Christ is not far off and that the end of all earthly things is in sight. In this chapter (3:2) the author confesses that he is of the generation which follows the apostles, and this seems proof positive that Peter could not have been the author, for he was certainly of the generation of the apostles, and followed only Christ. In addition, the author seems to be acquainted with other Christian writings.

199 What Christian writings did he know?

He quotes the transfiguration story as it is told by Matthew (compare II Peter 1:17, 18 with Matthew 17:5). He knows of John's Gospel (compare II Peter 1:14 with John 21:18, 19). He seems to have known something about a collection of Paul's letters (3:15-16) and may have known about Revelation and Hebrews.

200 Where was the book written?

No one knows, but the fact that the name of Peter was used, together with more or less vague references, suggests that it may have originated in Rome about A.D. 150.

201 What is the value of the book for modern Christians?

Like Juke, there is little in it of great moral and spiritual value, except for the fact that those who hold strongly to a belief in the second coming of Jesus find reasons for that belief in some passages from Second Peter. But it must be remembered that the author of the little book expected the second coming to occur very shortly, and at least seventeen hundred have elapsed since he expressed that confidence. The repetition of the material from Jude leaves the book with only a small amount of original material, and aside from some moral advice it has little value.

202 Why did he repeat the Jude material?

He was desperately concerned about maintaining the faith of the Church in the doctrine of the second coming, and the condemnation which Jude heaps on the Gnostics he appropriates to heap upon the Christians who were growing weak in that faith. Jude seems to have hoped to save the people he denounced, but the author of Second Peter seems to entertain no such confidence. The fact that he did not address his message to any one congregation, but to all the churches, seems to prove that he felt the apostasy was widespread and church-wide.

The thoughtful student can hardly have come to this point in the study without having recognized the fact that the early Christian Church was an extremely human institution. The membership was not made up exclusively of saints, nor were all its leaders wise. Very many of the same human problems which have to be met by modern churchmen had to be met by the first churchmen. The redemption of the world has not gone forward on the basis of miraculous interventions of divine power, but because the Spirit of God has worked continuously and triumphantly in the lives of "just men made perfect." At every age and under every circumstance God seems to have been prepared with an individual whom he has raised up to serve the cause and guide the Church. He has not left himself without a witness in any generation nor among any people. The leadership of the Holy Spirit is one of the most impressive evidences of the reality of our faith and the dependability of our witness.